The Urban Garden

The Urban Garden

How One Community Turned Idle Land into a Garden City
and How You Can, Too

JEREMY N. SMITH

FOREWORD BY
BILL McKIBBEN

PHOTOGRAPHS BY
CHAD HARDER AND **SEPP JANNOTTA**

Skyhorse Publishing

To Susan O'Connor and Crissie McMullan

10 9 8 7 6 5 4 3 2 1

The Library of Congress cataloged the hardcover edition as follows:

Smith, Jeremy N. Growing a garden city : how farmers, first graders, counselors, troubled teens, foodies, a homeless shelter chef, single mothers, and more are transforming themselves and their neighborhoods through the intersection of local agriculture and community—and how you can, too / Jeremy N. Smith ; foreword by Bill McKibben ; photographs by Chad Harder and Sepp Jannotta.
    p. cm.
"'How It Works' sections are based on and incorporate material originally prepared by Garden City Harvest."
ISBN 978-1-61608-108-9 (hardcover : alk. paper)
1. Community gardens—Montana—Missoula.
2. Community-supported agriculture—Montana—Missoula. I. Harder, Chad. II. Jannotta, Sepp. III. Title.

SB457.3.S64 2010
635.09786'85dc22
                            2010012369
Cover design by Danielle Ceccolini

Print ISBN: 978-1-62914-399-6
Ebook ISBN: 978-1-63220-168-3

Printed in China

Contents

Foreword

In January 2010, news came out that one in four American families experienced at least one day in 2009 when they were too short of money to buy the food they needed. That same week, different researchers released data revealing that a third of Americans were not just overweight but obese. It's easy to get discouraged.

But it's also easy, and important, to get encouraged.

This beautiful volume takes one small city, Missoula, Montana, and shows how it is learning to feed itself. Missoula residents are growing food so that even the neediest can eat and, in the process, are teaching their kids to grow the food so they'll have a way of providing for their families in the future.

This kind of urban/suburban farming builds community at least as effectively as soil, and that community is at least as important as the produce. If you've got a troubled teenager on your hands, he or she may well need to talk—but it will be easier to talk if you're stacking pumpkins at the same time, or pulling potatoes, or weeding carrots. If you want to connect one neighbor with another, it turns out that few things work better than starting a garden in the middle of the block. Everyone can do something: compost, water, kibitz.

The stories and pictures here speak for themselves. But it's important to know that the larger positive trends are not confined to Missoula.

After 150 years of decline, the number of farms in the country has started to grow rapidly in recent years. Most are small, producing local food for local people, not corn syrup for enormous processing factories. Young people are beginning to take up farming again in much greater numbers. There are still more prisoners than farmers in America—but the gap has begun to close. Farmers' markets are the fastest-growing part of the national food economy, with sales steadily increasing.

As you read this book, you'll start to see that change has come not just because it's needed, but because we've finally begun to understand that there's something in us that needs to nurture and provide. Sociologists not long ago found that shoppers at farmers' markets had ten times more conversations per visit than shoppers at supermarkets—it's a different world we've begun to build. Or maybe rebuild—because each picture in this book would be familiar to an American of a century ago, even if it seems unlikely to many of us at first glance.

Hooray for the good green thumbs of the Garden City. May their example continue to spread far and wide. We've never needed it more badly, or wanted it as much!

—**Bill McKibben**

The food bank really needed fresh food, and wouldn't it be a better experience for the university students if they knew that the food they were growing and working so hard for actually went to good hands? From there, we just kept casting the net wider and wider.

Josh Slotnick

After the military I went to college and studied philosophy. My partner at the time, Laurie, and I, we dug and planted a huge garden in our backyard in Pennsylvania. We were on an island of about four houses. Beyond that were two highways and a main road and an auto dealer. When we looked out all we saw was industrial craziness: smoke stacks, pavement, and bridges. I started making connections as to where it led.

Greg Price

We moved in about four years ago—Jason and I and my pregnant belly. We needed a bigger place because we were having this child, but we couldn't really afford a house and a yard. So we found this house without a yard, but we had this adjacent weed-infested dirt lot just staring at us in the face. It was forgotten city land.

Gita Saedi Kiely

My dad and I proceeded to have a screaming match in the eating area. Tim saw that we were obviously not getting anywhere because I was just enraged. Then we went for a walk, Tim and I, and he asked me if I wanted to be a part of Youth Harvest program, which would basically be me working up at a farm for a summer. And that's what I wanted. I was ready for my life to change.

Hannah Ellison

Introduction

Josh Slotnick started as an aspiring teacher offered the chance to feed the hungry. Greg Price was a military veteran determined to escape the "industrial craziness" of civilization as he knew it. Gita Saedi Kiely was a new homeowner and future mother staring out her window at a vacant lot. Hannah Ellison was a sixteen-year-old drug addict dragged 500 miles from home by a father desperate to save her life.

The way one local food organization in an unlikely location brought them and others together, what—united—they have been able to accomplish, and how other people all across the United States and around the world can transform themselves and their neighborhoods through the intersection of local agriculture and community are the subjects of this book. Each individual's story, accompanied by striking color photographs, informs, instructs, and, we hope, inspires. Taken as a whole, they prove it's possible to eat well locally even if you don't live on a rural homestead or in an elite urban area, and that volunteer-powered farms and gardens, even in a harsh climate, can provide satisfying food to feed a diverse population.

Even more important, they demonstrate that growing food, the most ancient of occupations, can address very modern social problems, from poverty and addiction to the sense of disconnection that is such a destructive part of contemporary life.

Garden City Harvest is a non-profit collaboration joining several small farms and community gardens in Missoula, Montana, a Rocky Mountain city of 68,000 where one in five residents lives in poverty. The needs are great, as are the challenges. To begin with, Missoula's frost-free growing season averages fewer than 100 days.

Nevertheless, Garden City Harvest's seven neighborhood-based farms and community gardens attract a far-ranging mix of area residents who purchase high-quality local organic food, rent a plot and grow their own vegetables, or "volunteer for veggies" by receiving free food in exchange for work. At these sites college students from the nearby University of Montana pursue graduate and undergraduate coursework in environmental studies; 2,000 area children visit annually on field trips; and, in cooperation with the local youth drug court, troubled teenagers find a positive environment and professional therapy.

But perhaps the most impressive feat is how the organization changes and is changed by its participants.

Elementary school students arriving on field trips delight in meeting the sow and three growing piglets fed by their daily lunch scraps. Teen addicts joining in "farm therapy" not only support one another and fellow farm workers, but also organize and run a special mobile farmers' market for seniors who could not otherwise enjoy fresh local food. College students learning how to farm discover that they are role models and mentors to those same teens and essential suppliers to the individuals and families served by the area food bank, homeless shelter, and youth homes. Strangers participating in community gardens to grow their own food form unexpected new friendships and enlarge one another's sense of neighborhood. Moreover, the farms and gardens become a gathering place for cultural and artistic events, from potluck suppers and celebrations to concerts, lectures, and readings.

All these efforts produce tangible results: Each year more than 100,000 pounds of healthy, high-quality food is grown to feed those in need, all while educating the larger public about local, sustainable food systems.

Fifteen years ago, Garden City Harvest, its farms, and all but two of its garden sites did not even exist. Today it represents one of the country's most far-reaching experiments in community-based agriculture.

Like "hope" or "freedom," "community" can be a vague word, meaning different things to different people. In its most basics sense, however, community means interdependence. Each member relies, at least in part, on the others. Everyone is necessary. Everyone belongs. Based on this simple but powerful principle, the successful practices of Garden City Harvest can take root anywhere.

What's special wherever you live, as here, is how you grow.

—Jeremy N. Smith

Com•mu•ni•ty Sup•port•ed Ag•ri•cul•ture (abbr. **CSA**) *n.* **1.** A farm subscription. Members pay up-front for a weekly share of an area farm's seasonal harvest, supporting local agriculture in exchange for choice food. **2.** "Food with the farmer's face on it."

Ag•ri•cul•ture Sup•port•ed Com•mu•ni•ty *n.* **1.** A community bound to one another by local food and farming. Such a group often encompasses diverse members and multiple locations and projects, each undertaken to improve lives and create individual connections. **2.** "The new faces of local food."

BREAKING
GROUND

IF ONE IMAGE OF THE UNIVERSITY IS AN IVORY *tower isolated from its surrounding community, its antithesis must be the student farm. At sites like the PEAS Farm, co-managed by Garden City Harvest and the University of Montana Environmental Studies Program, course work is valued not just as a formal learning exercise or a letter grade on a transcript, but also for the vital nourishment—tens of thousands of pounds of fresh local organic produce—it provides to people in need.*

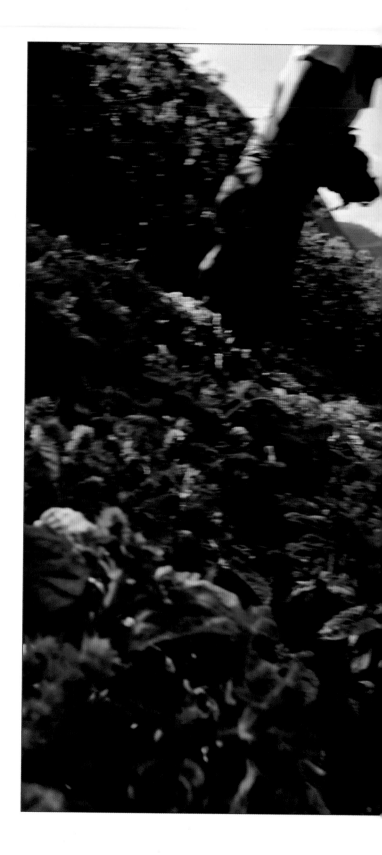

The Founder:

Josh Slotnick

PEAS Farm Director

"Working on a small farm like this you realize over a little bit of time that you are necessary. . . . You realize that you can actually make a change in the world."

Father, farmer, teacher, community leader. Co-founder.

Following college and a stint in the Peace Corps, Josh Slotnick entered a six-month program at the University of California, Santa Cruz called the Apprenticeship in Ecological Horticulture. "There was a student farm where you worked and lived, and I loved it," he says. "You knew what it was like to belong and be personally effective."

He married Kim Murchison, a fellow Santa Cruz student, and the couple moved to Missoula and started their own small-scale organic vegetable farm, Clark Fork Organics. After they had the first of three children, Slotnick panicked: "I dragged my family off to Cornell in Ithaca, New York, for the graduate program in international agriculture." When an initial plan to study international development soured, he was pushed by his wife to think more broadly: What was he interested in? What spoke to him? What mattered? "That learning experience in Santa Cruz, that was it," he says. "What would it take for me to work for a place like that?"

Everything is serendipity. In 1996, a new Farm Bill passed, which ended "welfare as we know it." This meant cutoff dates on food stamps and aid to families with dependent children. Suddenly the Missoula Food Bank and WIC [Women, Infants, and Children nutrition] program were overwhelmed. Meanwhile, I had just returned to Missoula after finishing graduate school and resumed work at my family farm. Deborah Slicer, who teaches philosophy at the university, came by to learn more about organic gardening and we became friends. She read my thesis about student farms where sustainable agriculture was taught through a blend of hands-on work and traditional academics and said, "Why don't we do this here?" I said, "Well, you're the professor on the inside. Why don't we?"

Mary Pittaway, who ran WIC, and Caitlin DeSilvey, the director of the Missoula Urban Demonstration Project, began a series of conversations with us. The food bank really needed fresh food, they said, and wouldn't it be a better experience for the university students if they knew that the food they were growing and working so hard for actually went to good hands? From there, we all kept casting the net wider and wider. We had people join us from the school district, from the university, from any agency or nonprofit that wanted to move into discussions and fill up white boards with ideas. We did this for about six months and winnowed our work down to one issue. The issue was food security.

Food security, as we decided, meant two things. One, people would have access to food. They would know they could eat tomorrow and the next day and the next. Two, the production of food would be similarly available. The way we produced food now would also enable us to produce food in the future. Part of this would be a student farm where we would teach participants how to farm, promise the food bank a set number of pounds of food, and sell shares in a CSA [community supported agriculture program—see page 108 for a fuller explanation] as an income generator. Another part would be community gardens in neighborhoods where people didn't have money or access to land. Because if you don't have money and you don't have access to land, you're going to be hungry.

With these two programs—a student farm and neighborhood community gardens—Garden City Harvest was born. My role was to be the farm director.

We started the farm out at Fort Missoula, which is an obscure location. People know where it is, but nobody walks by there, which in a sense was good for us because our mistakes were not seen. Our first season, there were thirty students. We had just two acres and a CSA of twenty-five to thirty people, most of them WIC clients. It took about three years before we could sell all our CSA shares, but we met our obligations, and we gave food to the food bank, and the fields looked beautiful in a spot nestled against the Bitterroot River. I felt passion, and it was real.

In 2001, we moved. The university decided they had a new use for the land we were on. The president's executive assistant called me one day and said, "You better find a new place. We're not kicking you out today, but the writing is on the wall. Don't say you weren't warned. Don't give me that bleeding-heart crap." [Laughs] He was a great no-nonsense guy.

I was upset, but I couldn't be mad, because at the time, though we had been successful and created a following, most people at the university didn't know what we did. Now there is an emphasis on sustainable food and farming here in the UM Environmental Studies Program and at thousands of other colleges. Then it was nothing. I was this weird skinny guy on the other side of town beating the earth with a stick. No one really knew we were there, and I didn't know that we should have been doing anything other than the thing we were doing.

I put the word out among all the people that I knew: "We're going to need a place." Dave Harmon, the neighbor to the north of what is now the PEAS Farm, called me and said, "Come check out this piece of land." So we went up there and dug around, expecting rocks because there are rocks in that area, but it was really nice, beautiful soil in a very open,

public place, where people walk by on a trail or drive by in cars. Dave has great skills at brokering deals, and he got the school district, which owns the land, to lease it to the city. The city then subleased half the property—a six-plus-acre field—to Garden City Harvest.

Over a year and a half, we moved the farm, which was when we jumped from a marginal to a public operation. It wasn't just that we had a new site. Moving was an opportunity to raise money and raise awareness about our whole effort. We raised $50,000 and just hit the ground running. We put up a fence and greenhouse; we built sheds; we took a six-plus-acre field of knap-weed and made it beautiful. There was a great groundswell of enthusiasm. As a big community project, we built a straw-bale, post-and-beam structure with recycled, salvaged lumber to store and distribute food. I realized that community supported agriculture is where a community of people band together to support a farm, but the PEAS Farm also worked the opposite way. We agriculturally supported the community.

We start work at the end of February by making potting soil, filling up trays, and sowing seeds. To prepare the field, we spread compost and till it in and make beds. The seeds that we sow grow into starts, which are little baby plants we then transplant out into the field. We also do some direct seeding—things like beans, corn, peas, radishes, carrots, and beets—where we put the seeds right into the ground with a seeder. Once everything's in, we move irrigation pipe. Water hits the ground and the race is on between the weeds and the plants we want. The starting gun is the irrigation. Nothing grows until you hit it with water. Then it all takes off.

I work all the time. It's been hard on my back and my shoulders and my marriage and my psyche, but I love it, too. Mix physical engagement with a feeling of community, humble work with tangible results, and the barriers between people erode. Weed carrots on your hands and knees with someone for four hours, at the end you know where they went to high school, and you've probably heard a story about a girlfriend or a boyfriend or parent or what they did last summer. Now do that day after day and our students become a tribe. They belong to each other, to the place, and to the activity. Working on a small farm like this, you realize over a little bit of time that you are necessary. Without you, the carrots won't be weeded as well—or maybe at all. And then when you weed the carrots, they grow beautifully and you bring them to the food bank, and you see that you've been personally effective. You realize that you can actually make a change in the world.

We grow. It evolves. The first program born out of this, over time, was Youth Harvest, where a small group of teenagers in the Missoula County Youth Drug Court have the option to work at the PEAS Farm. They get paid and we have a licensed professional counselor on staff who oversees them. The kids are integrated with the PEAS students and they spend the summer working here. It's a transformative experience. All their lives they've been unnecessary and in the way and causing trouble. The opportunity for them to walk tall and think about ownership is huge. It doesn't always work on all kids but it works often enough. As with the PEAS students, it serves as a reference point for what they do with the rest of their lives. They come back and say, "This was the coolest thing I ever did."

We get close to 2,000 kids a year up on field trips to the farm. This started because a teacher called me and said, "Can I bring my students up?" I said, "Sure." And then another one called and another one called. I couldn't teach the PEAS students and then run back to the first graders and then back again, so a graduate student focusing on environmental education created our Community Education Program to schedule and conduct farm field trips and summer camps, and to help organize school gardens and after-school programs. Now university students interested in environmental education learn how to do science lessons around the farm with kindergarteners and first, second, and third graders, then meet once a week to review and critique each other's performance as teachers.

I think the town needed to have a public farm. People drive by, they walk by, they come here, and they congregate. It's part of the public sphere and public dialogue and culture. Neighbors bring their kids to play in the playground. We have special events and two hundred people come. They walk by our beds and they notice things. People tell me that they see the farm from the saddle of Mount Jumbo and have a better idea what time of the year it is. "Oh, look, it's greened up." "Oh, they're harvesting the winter squash." "Oh, look, the orchard is in bloom." We added 3.25 acres to our 6.5 acres. We built a chicken coop and now we have laying hens. A couple years ago we started raising three pigs twice a year. Nearby there's Rattlesnake Elementary School, right across the creek, and each day our students bike food waste from the school cafeteria to the farm. The pigs eat food that would otherwise go into the landfill. We eat one pig and send one pig to the food bank and sell our third pig to a neighbor to cover all the costs.

Two years ago there was an apple on the cover of *Time* with the word "local" over the word "organic." "Is local the new organic?" the caption said. None of us knew this wave was coming. We weren't geniuses who could foretell the future. We were just at the right place at the right time. But what we were doing was the local instantiation, not a national trend, which makes people feel like they are kind of with it. They don't say, "Oh, that could happen in California, it could never happen here." They read about it and they're like, "Oh, yeah, we've got that, too."

A SUCCESSFUL COMMUNITY WELCOMES AND

rewards more than one kind of person. Diverse residents support themselves and enrich one another's lives with different talents. So, too, over a season's communal work at a student farm, a group bonds to become a family.

The Student:

Cori Ash

PEAS Student

"In every job I was producing real things I could put my hands around. Pulling carrots or picking kale, I felt something bigger than myself. A good life will include work that feels necessary, and if everybody's got to eat, someone needs to grow food."

PEAS stands for the Program in Ecological Agriculture and Society, supervised, for-credit spring, summer, and fall internships on the 9.75-acre PEAS Farm, two miles from the University of Montana campus, under Environmental Studies Program faculty member and Garden City Harvest co-founder Josh Slotnick. The organic food produced—over 40,000 pounds a year—goes to customers of a weekly community supported agriculture (CSA) program, clients of the Missoula Food Bank and other emergency food shelters, and low-income senior citizen shoppers at the Mobile Market run by Youth Harvest Program participants.

"Producing a quality product was a real obligation that I enjoyed fulfilling," says Cori Ash. "I grew up in a fairly affluent town in New Jersey, but my dad was a mechanic, driving a beater Suburban around to pick up his kids. By his own labor, he survived and raised a good family. I've always felt proud of him. I wanted to feel proud of the work that I did and feel like I worked hard for it, too."

I went to college in New Jersey at a little liberal arts school, majoring in environmental studies, and I took classes in Costa Rica and in Utah and Arizona before dropping out of school and moving to South Carolina and North Carolina. When I was twenty-one, I got married and moved out to Whitefish, Montana, with my newly attached husband. I worked in coffee shops as a cook for a couple of years. I taught yoga for a couple of years. I worked in a day care at the ski mountain for a lift ticket. When I started working for a woman who had a farm in Whitefish, I fell in love with farming, but I realized what a hard way it was to make a living. In the fall of 2006, I came to Missoula for college. I was twenty-five, about to separate from my husband, and I decided to take the PEAS internship.

Day one was a CSA pickup day. I showed up at nine in the morning and there were no real introductions. I just got tossed with everybody else into harvesting. Josh Slotnick, being the highly busy man that he is, didn't know that I'd just come from managing a farm. I remember him coming out and showing me and some other girls how to dig potatoes. In my mind I was thinking, "I just spent the last month and a half digging potatoes. I know how to dig potatoes." [Laughs]

But it was good for me, really checking my own ego, going through that sometimes-painful experience of being the new person in town. Things were different and I was seeing different methods. Just digging potatoes, we were using pitchforks—well, I had always dug potatoes with a shovel. I remember being a little awkward, talking with the other students, and them asking, "Is this one okay? Is this one?" And trying to say, subtly, "Yeah, I think that one is a good one," based on experience, but not wanting to be the girl who thought she could do it all.

In the fall class, every intern worked two three-hour shifts a week, Monday and Thursday, and then Wednesday afternoons everyone came together for a class lecture or farm tour or other group activity. In the summer class, which I took, too, work days were Monday through Thursday, eight or nine AM to noon; then Friday we had a lecture in the morning and a field trip in the afternoon. If it was early spring, Josh talked about starting plants in the greenhouse and the benefits of transplanting versus direct seeding. A week later the topic was the parts and pieces of irrigation—flood irrigation, overhead irrigation, drip irrigation—and how they work together. Maybe a couple weeks later we were talking about soils, pests, and water use, then season extenders and Reemay [blankets]. During the fall, we had a class on orchards and fruit production. On field trips, we went to a farm started by a former PEAS student, a farm trying to have a CSA on a sliding scale, an innovative big grain farm, and a peach orchard. We were there for a couple of hours, so we might see a little technique, but really we were hearing someone's story. I got a sense of the lives of people in the area farming for a living and all the small things that come together to make it work. I asked myself, how could that translate to my life?

Some PEAS students had been in Missoula and knew each other. Other people got to know each other through work, and that's how I did it. That first fall, getting plants out of the field, breaking down drip and irrigation lines, or cleaning out the greenhouse, I could spend an entire morning with the same three people. We talked about both our work and our personal lives and what we struggled with. It was technical stuff like how and why we move plants, and it was, "Where am I going? What am I going to do? Who am I going to do it with?" That year was a big time of adjustment for me. After being married for four years, I was going through leaving my husband, and this was the first place I'd ever moved to on my own. I definitely had walls up, protecting myself, feeling like that shy kid on the outskirts of the group, but harvesting and breaking down the field together, I came to feel comfortable with the other students. Sharing stories, solving roadblocks, spending that much time together every day, we got to know each other in an intimate way.

The beauty of the place was that everyone was learning together and finding his or her own voice. There was no right or wrong way to do something, just what worked for you and what didn't. My first semester, about ten other PEAS students and I did the sustainable agriculture education practicum, in which public school classes came to the farm and we led field trips. One day, I led a kids' field trip through the harvested cabbage aisles, changed the starter in one of the trucks with Josh, and then biked

down to campus, and I thought, "I just learned so much more this morning than I'm going to learn in a normal classroom." We always had six different projects going on, and in every job I was producing real things I could put my hands around. Pulling carrots or picking kale, I felt something bigger than myself. A good life will include work that feels necessary, and if everybody's got to eat, someone needs to grow food.

As time progressed, the people who wanted to be there most couldn't ask enough questions. We wanted to get deeper and deeper into everything. People got ideas: a better way to manage the chickens, a new method of weeding onions, planting trees along the river trail behind the hoop houses—even building housing so that we could all be up there all the time! The pigs were somebody's idea. Off and on over the years, there have been bees. [Community Education Program Director] Jason Mandala is trying dry-land farming. Sometimes an idea creates disasters, and then you have a swath full of weeds and no one's got the time to take care of it, but the nature of the place was that if someone wanted to put their heart into a project and see it through, the space and support were there.

It challenged me to be in a position of responsibility. I can remember days thinking very clearly, "Oh, my Lord, we're balancing so many things here! We're trying to be productive! We're trying to be educational!" You had the hearts and minds and energy of excited young people coming together, but we still had to produce wonderful food.

Whether it was the first baby carrots of the year or the last of a crop of cabbages, it felt good to know that people were eating something that I'd put my heart into. I knew that I was sending a family away with a bag of peas that they were going to eat before they even got home because the kids were so psyched about it. Once or twice a week we took food down to the food bank, and harvesting winter squash we'd start a "fire line," where people cut these big beautiful multicolored vegetables and then threw them down the line to the back of a pickup truck. We worked until we couldn't load any more, and looking at that food, I knew that I was a part of it—from

ordering to harvesting. I had done what I needed to do. Now the food was on its own journey, and that was powerful for me.

I've come to believe that there's a direct correlation between the quality of a plant and how it was produced. We spent entire days bent over, picking things that on the open market were going to go for seventy cents a pound, but if romance budded during the pruning of the tomatoes, I think that love transferred into each bite. At the PEAS Farm, the hands of twenty-five people might have come into contact with a crop of broccoli, and all the while they were talking philosophy or making jokes or just being humans together. People eating those vegetables were sharing that happiness. When I was in my late teens and early twenties, I would go into a food store or a little organic market and be blown away by the prices. I just couldn't bring myself to spend that kind of money on peas. After a season working on a farm, it was like, "Clearly this is where you spend your money. If you're going to spend it anywhere, you spend it on food that you know was grown well, with heart and soul put into the work, when you can be happy with the hard life you're supporting and how the land was treated."

Spend a full season with a group of people and you make yourselves a family. Because we were strong women, excited about life, proudly doing something we loved, the other PEAS women and I became examples to the teenage girls working alongside us in the Youth Harvest program. Especially at seventeen, especially if you've been in trouble, you're looking for a life that speaks to you. You want to know how to dive deep into a skill and share your passion, whatever it is, with other people. When I was seventeen, I know I didn't see people trying to live their dreams and follow their hearts, and when one particular student showed up in all white—white eyeliner, white jeans, pale complexion—without a smile on her face, I became her mentor. Making a trip to town to go pick up pig food, for example, I'd say, "Rhonda, why don't you come take a ride with me?" Along the way we'd talk about music or boyfriends or whatever was going on in her life. As a mentor, I didn't necessarily share a whole lot of my personal history, but I was the objective listener to her story. She had come here as some kind of "troubled youth" and of course she had authority issues, but I remember having conversations with her, saying, "Not everyone is looking to power trip over you. There are people out there who are interested and concerned and respect you." And she said to me, "I know. There's people like you."

I left the farm last September, traveled for a couple of months, and came back feeling lost. It was a big transition period in my life and all the people that I turned to for support, whether it was for housing or to go out and get a beer with me, were farming people. Even right now, I'm without a home. There hasn't been a night when I haven't got a phone call saying, "Cori, come stay at our house. We're making dinner." It's about more than just the time we spent together. Our hearts connected. I can sit on the porch with someone I farmed with and know they understand the feeling of having so much of yourself that you want to put into things and struggling with how exactly to do that.

Largely because I enjoyed working with the Youth Harvest kids, I'm working for a wilderness therapy program, but I miss farm work. I was down in the desert in Idaho in early May, and, as the land started greening up, I felt this physical pull towards the potatoes and alfalfa fields. My hope is that I'll find that balance the PEAS Farm showed me, where I can grow food with other people in a space we share for mentorship. No one can run an entire farm alone. Someone needs to be really good at the tractor and someone needs to be really good in the greenhouse. We can help each other, and if you try to do it all yourself, whether it's your life or your farm, it's going to be lonely, hard, and a lot less fun. Already I can't drive anywhere without checking out someone's irrigation lines. [Laughs] I think, "That thing is busted. He's got to stick a wire in it, and it'll be working fine."

AS PLANTS PROPAGATE THEMSELVES BY SPREADING *seeds, teachers disseminate their ideas through students. When the classroom includes the entire community, teachers become mentors and students become leaders.*

The Teacher:

Neva Hassanein

University of Montana Professor of Environmental Studies

"Combine everyone's actions and you get this cascade. As more and more people grow even a little bit of their own food and disconnect from that dominant system, they build an alternative system that I hope will flourish in its own right."

"EVST 225—Community and Environment. EVST 450—Food, Agriculture, and the Environment. EVST 495—Women, Environment, and Social Change. EVST 520—Environmental Organizing. EVST 555—Research Methods for Social Change. EVST 594—The Politics of Food. EVST 594—Assessing the Food System."

Neva Hassanein's interdisciplinary courses at the University of Montana focus on social change and local, sustainable alternatives to the conventional industrial food system. Many of her students complement these classes with Garden City Harvest/Environmental Studies Program PEAS Farm internships.

"Universities have often set up a false distance between academics and the rest of society," she says. "I research and teach because I want to make a difference in other people's lives."

Right now, a handful of huge global agribusiness and agrichemical corporations really control our food supply. They make decisions in boardrooms far away that have the capacity to affect all of us. Industrial agriculture produces so much food and distributes it through a vast network, yet communities are recognizing that we're literally putting all of our eggs in one basket. Last year we saw incredibly high fuel prices lead to incredibly high food prices. Don't we want to retain some capacity to produce food locally?

On the simplest level, what Garden City Harvest does is create an opportunity for everyone who wants to grow food to do it. When most people first get interested in growing their own food, it's less political than personal. Gardening, you connect with nature and develop some degree of self-reliance. It's great outdoor exercise. You can freeze, can, or dry the food you harvest. You can prepare a meal and share it with friends. Your own small garden plot isn't going to change the world. But combine everyone's actions and you get this cascade. As more and more people grow even a little bit of their own food and disconnect from that dominant system, they build an alternative system that I hope will flourish in its own right. In that sense, Garden City Harvest farms and gardens are symbols for transformation in the whole community.

The university is a major partner because of the PEAS program. At the farm, our students learn how to grow high-quality produce, but they also learn a new way of organizing things. They know what's happening with the industrial system. Historically, we grew much of our own food, but now only about 10 percent of what Montanans eat is from Montana. Of 60 million acres of land in agriculture here, the vast majority produce raw commodities shipped out of state or even out of the country to be processed. Meanwhile, we have high rates of hunger and poverty.

Students see that they can make a difference. The food that they grow goes to the Missoula Food Bank. What they're doing makes a meaningful contribution. At the same time, they see people like Josh Slotnick who are committing their lives to

a just, sustainable food system. They come to see that they, too, have a unique style of leadership. They start to bust open these cultural myths that we have about who creates change and how change is created.

Since 1997, over a thousand students have gone through the PEAS program. For the first time for many of them, they gain a sense of efficacy and confidence in their ability to solve daunting problems. Environmental studies can be a depressing subject; there's a lot that's wrong in the world today. What PEAS does is give young people hope for the future. Students are growing vegetables, but they're also connecting with and learning from and challenging each other. Harvesting carrots all morning, they exchange ideas and form their own opinions.

These are the next generation of environmental leaders. A couple of the women working on the farm went on to create the University of Montana Farm to College Program, where the university buys local and regional food to serve in the dining halls. One of those [women] went on to work for a coalition that promotes policies in Montana that will further local food systems as a form of economic development. The other is helping promote alternative farming systems to get away from the use of chemicals in agriculture. The person who was the development director for Garden City Harvest for several years had gone though our program. Another of our graduates runs the Community Education Program. Former students are starting farms and supporting farms, farmers, and farmland preservation from Oregon to Vermont. Several others are members of the Montana Legislature. They've made simple, practical policy changes to connect local producers with each other and local consumers.

This is important, exciting work. It inspires our students to see their peers or people who are not much older than themselves become leaders. It inspires those of us who are older to see this younger generation coming in behind us. Social movements are about a sense of belonging. Those who share certain values recognize that they're not alone. The farms and gardens link people to this place and to each other. They can talk about food issues and deliberate and make decisions. They can take specific actions to control more of their food supply from its production to its consumption. Together they put in hours and hours of work toward a vibrant local system that can provide a greater portion of our food, reduce transportation costs and pollution, and create and nurture important relationships between people. I get my satisfaction seeing their energy and passion. Because of our students and former students I know that the world will be a better place.

Is community supported agriculture perfect? No. We can't claim that it alters the underlying condition that creates hunger and food insecurity, which is poverty. But local farms and gardens help us take a step towards self-reliance and equality. If everyone has a right to eat healthy, high-quality food, we need to have a greater sense of where our food is going to come from in the future for people of all income levels. We have to have active, informed citizens, consumers, farmers, and food processors. We need new policies, we need new forms of education, and we need new food-system infrastructure. We need Garden City Harvest.

NEVA HASSANEIN

IN A COLD CLIMATE, THE GROWING SEASON *ends in October and may not resume again until May. Because a community never closes, however, neither does a community farm.*

The Caretaker:

Rick White

PEAS Farm Caretaker

"You get the view and the ten acres of gorgeous scenery. You get the porch swing and the creek outside your back door and the mountains outside your front gate. And you get the community that comes with it."

Rick White grew up and went to college in northeast and central Arkansas. In February 2008, he moved to Missoula to enter the graduate program in environmental studies at the University of Montana. "One icy, snow-covered day in March, I hiked to a mountaintop and saw a two-story straw-bale barn with giant eaves under a sharply sloping silver metal roof, nestled between Mount Jumbo to the east, Waterworks Hill to the west, the Rattlesnake Wilderness to the north, and the center of town to the south," he says. "From a distance, prayer flags flew and a cold wind blew a foot of snow on the ground. It was the most beautiful setting for a small farm that I'd ever seen."

Six months later it was home.

The first day after I'd moved in, I woke early. I had some more moving to do and I was really happy to be here and I walked downstairs just to take it all in. Outside there were two girls my age who I didn't know. They had met here to go on their Sunday morning run. It was 6:30 AM. They were on my porch. [Laughs] That was my transition into caretaking.

Community is the defining characteristic of the farm. It's a unique public place. Even if I'm in a towel just out of the shower it's okay for people to walk in my kitchen door. The nature of this position and my place within the community and within the organization is point person. Throughout the year, at all hours of the day, people drop in and ask questions: "How do I get a share in the CSA?" "Can you tell me more about this farm?" "My son is a student here at the university and he wants to get involved. What does he need to do?" "Can I pick all your cucumbers?" "Can I volunteer in exchange for some food?"

My responsibility is to make sure that they walk away with a good experience. As a community farm, we're a hybrid between a private farm, a city park, and a YMCA. That doesn't mean you can come and pick any vegetables that you want. It's structured and organized, not a free-for-all. But our mission, roughly stated, is that we want to grow good food for people in need, and we want to encourage participation by all. If you're new to the idea of community supported agriculture or you want to know about the PEAS Program, I can talk to you about it. If you want to volunteer, I can tell you how. It's not a requirement of the caretaker position, but I've taken some visitors on walking tours or had them come with me while I was working. In the process, I get to meet and know people of all shapes and sizes, from all over town, from the bottom classes of society to the most affluent.

I love the give and take. As caretaker, you get the view and the ten acres of gorgeous scenery. You get the porch swing and the creek outside your back door and the mountains outside your front gate. And you get the community that comes with it. The farm is an idyllic spot. It has scenic vistas, great soil, and great water. We keep the gates open because we want people to experience it.

Parents looking for something to do with their kids for an afternoon bring their children up to see the animals. They come and feed the pigs and play on the playground and spend an hour or two here. They're not CSA members; they're not recipients of the food bank. They're just neighbors. The playground has nothing to do with farming, but it has everything to do with what we think a community farm should be. In the same way, PEAS students and former PEAS students are very attached to the farm. Most are close friends. They'll hang out with me and my dog on the porch, and we'll talk about what we're doing and our passions— one of which is sustainable agriculture.

The actual requirements of the job vary seasonally, as does all farm work. In the spring, I have a full load of classes, so I go to and from campus, but on the farm we mix and pot soil, take seeds, go through the binder of all of our farm plans for the year, and accordingly plant, water, and get the season started in the green-house. When the summer comes, we move out into the fields and it's chaos and happiness, exhilaration and exhaustion. You just run and do as much as you can in the short time you have: preparing the fields, moving water lines, planting, weeding, harvesting, and helping get the CSA ready for pickup and delivery. And

then, in the fall, you frantically try to put up food for the winter. In November and December we make compost, put up irrigation lines, plant garlic, and order all the seeds for next year. We installed a pellet stove. We're going to put in a big kitchen cabinet. Other little projects keep the pipes from freezing.

It's home maintenance, basically, but on a farm. Summer days the kitchen floor is dirty and I have a sink full of dirty dishes that other people didn't wash. I didn't get them dirty, but it's still my responsibility to clean them. In the winter, when it snows, I plow the parking lot with a tractor. I open and close the gate. Twice a day I feed and water three pigs and thirty chickens. Things break and I have to fix them. Things fall apart and then I have to put them back together. Most of the pig food we get from Rattlesnake Elementary School, for example. Monday through Friday, the elementary school kids dump their food waste out after lunch, and we collect it in a two-foot-tall, fifteen-by-thirty-inch tub that we haul in a bike trailer across the bridge over Rattlesnake Creek. Well, today the wheels came off one of the garbage cans and I dumped a good ninety pounds of pizza sopping wet with chocolate milk in the parking lot. [Laughs] I picked it all up by hand, put it back into the can, hauled it back here, and finished my duties.

Everything here is built simply for rough use: open shelving, no carpets, a bathroom with a stand-up shower and toilet and sink. Adjacent to the kitchen is our main room with huge, bay, barn double doors, and a large picnic table with four benches. There, in the summer, PEAS students have lunch together, and there we weigh, measure, sort, and separate all of our vegetables for CSA pickups. From nails in the rafters we string, braid, and hang garlic and peppers to dry. Upstairs, in the storage loft, we hang thousands and thousands of pounds of onions and it looks like a jungle. The last room on the second floor is my bedroom. In ten by twelve feet, I've got a bed, my bookshelves, my guitar, my harmonica, and my laptop. My dog Finn, a bluetick hound crossed with a German shorthaired pointer from the humane society, sleeps with me. Out the window I see the north part of the farm and the Rattlesnake Wilderness.

I think a lot of people anticipate it being lonely, but I wouldn't trade this for an apartment or a dorm or any other option. I took the job in the first place because as caretaker I get to experience the after-hours and all the seasons, not just 8 AM to noon, Monday through Thursday, spring, summer, or fall. Those long Missoula days when the sun doesn't go down until 10:30 PM are intoxicating. Fall comes and I enjoy the yellows and the oranges of the season while they last. In the winter I'm cooped up like the chickens, but the living is good. I like the solitude. I love the quiet reflection. There's a lot of music and a lot of lying around my room reading and watching movies on my computer.

Last week, January 9th, I had my first visitors of the year. I was coming down the stairs on my way to go pick up pig food from Rattlesnake School when a father and son came in the kitchen door. The father had read Michael Pollan's letter to the president in the *New York Times* and found it very intriguing. Now he and his son, who's a student, were interested in what Garden City Harvest has to offer. I'd spent a month in almost total solitude and that kind of jarred me back into reality.

In another year and a half I finish my master's degree in environmental studies. Whether or not I stay on as caretaker, I think I'll go into research and, after graduation, carry that on to PhD work and teaching or leading another program like PEAS based on my experience here. Before, I had some agricultural experience, but I couldn't run my own farm. I didn't have very strong plant knowledge. I couldn't tell you all the different cycles of a weed or when to use the spader or the mower or the harrow or the bucket on the tractor. My first summer, I was learning right alongside the other interns, and I'm still a PEAS student. The hands-on nature of farming continues to capture my imagination and my attention. Having tangible physical labor attached to an alternative idea brings people very close very quickly as a group. I always want to have that passion and mission.

In the spring out my window I'll see snow melt and life emerge with the mud. The sky will be blue and not so gray. Towards the end of spring, it'll be green and people will be happy and active without all their winter layers of clothing on. It'll be a new experience. I'll lose my precious solitude and love it anyway.

How It Works

Student Farm

Student farms combine traditional academics with hands-on work at a farm located near campus and community. Many produce fruits and vegetables for donation or sale. In the process, participants learn by doing, may earn wages or class credit, and nourish people and the land.

Background

Student farms come in many varieties. Organizers may pay students to work, operate exclusively with volunteers, or require tuition fees in exchange for instruction and class credit. Some farms exist only for students and faculty; others, like the Garden City Harvest PEAS Farm, are closely attached to the non-campus community. Moreover, farms may have real production obligations, as is the case with the PEAS Farm's commitments to the Missoula Food Bank, Youth Harvest Mobile Market, and a community supported agriculture (CSA) program.

Learning in this situation is akin to learning a foreign language through immersion, says instructor and farm director Josh Slotnick. "[Students] are shown what to do and why, but an understanding of the big picture comes only over the course of the summer," he says. "Work on the farm with your eyes open, ask lots of questions, and by August you 'get it.'"

PEAS stands for the Program in Ecological Agriculture and Society. Students are involved in all phases of the farm, from greenhouse work in February to selling pumpkins in October. Farm work is humble labor, and this kind of shared experience breaks down the barriers that typically separate people. As they acquire new skills and make a meaningful contribution to their community, students come to see themselves and their peers as leaders.

Seasonal Internships

PEAS internships, available fall, summer, and spring for both undergraduate and graduate credit at the University of Montana, change with the seasons:

- Spring Session: Labor on the farm begins in late February. In the greenhouse, students make potting mixes, planting flats, and greenhouse benches; sow seeds and transplant stock; and take care of general spring upkeep on the farm. As the weather warms and they work outside, they learn about biological and horticultural topics pertinent to raising and maintaining produce, herbs, and flowers. The class considers fertility and soil health, weed management, preventative as well as curative pest control, and farm planning. They share weekend watering responsibilities for the field and greenhouse.
- Summer Session: The summer program combines four days of farming with a formal class and a field trip on the fifth day. Each Friday a different subject is addressed in lecture, and Monday though Thursday, 8 AM to noon, students do the work necessary to run a diverse and productive organic farm.

As the summer progresses, students gain an appreciation for the tight western Montana growing season and learn some strategies to work within those limits.

They assume more roles and responsibilities, and by classes' end know the major vegetable crop families and understand their culture; are familiar with common techniques for building soil, managing weeds, and dealing with local pest populations; and are well acquainted with the technical challenges growers face. "The educational aim is not to provide universal and definitive answers to those issues," says Slotnick, "but rather to gain an understanding of the issues themselves."

• Fall Session: Work on the farm continues immediately after school starts and lasts through Halloween. Until the first frost, students focus on harvesting to supply a CSA, the Youth Harvest Mobile Market, and the Missoula Food Bank.

Students in the fields >>

Producing Relationships

Work at a student farm is most satisfying when participants come together. Every day in the summer, two PEAS students make lunch for the rest of class from the morning's harvest. "Everybody set out the food and plates, and we chatted about what was going on in the field and in our lives, recharging and reconnecting after spending the morning working," says former PEAS student Cori Ash. "I could have been weeding or braiding onions or planting broccoli or seeding in the greenhouse. At lunch I sat next to whoever was working on the tractor or laying irrigation and caught up: 'How was your morning? How are things looking over there?' It reminded all of us that we were working towards a common goal."

The PEAS Farm collaborates to grow. Through the program, Garden City Harvest and the University of Montana Environmental Studies Program have created valuable and unique partnerships with each other and the community. "Environmental Studies provides the labor for the program in the form of the students," says Josh Slotnick. "Garden City Harvest comes up with the operating expenses to run a farm." CSA members buy seasonal shares of the farm's produce, which helps to fund some basic operating costs. Another major partner is the Missoula Food Bank, where most of the farm's production goes to provide high-quality food to low-income people. Local government also plays a role because the farm is subleased from the City of Missoula, which leases the land from the Missoula County Public School District. Area schoolchildren visit the farm on field trips and, through their lunch scraps, supply some of the feed for its animals.

Going public established the farm as a full-fledged member of the community. In 2001, after five years using temporary university land, the PEAS Farm moved to its current location in Missoula's Rattlesnake Valley, supported by donations from the city, university, local businesses, civic groups, and family foundations and trusts. Now nearly ten acres—including a playground, straw-bale barn, and open space for community gatherings—the PEAS Farm welcomes students and local residents alike.

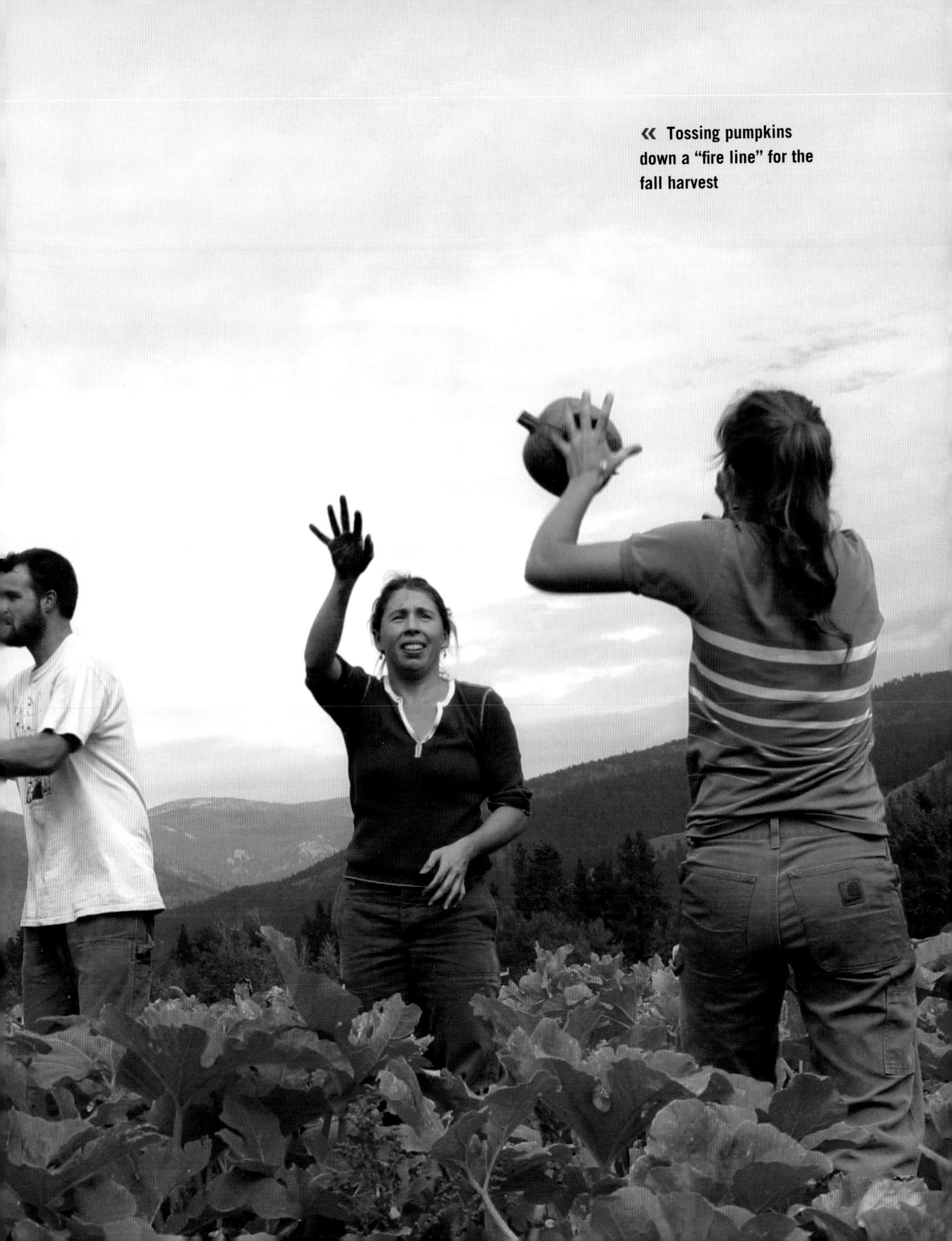

« Tossing pumpkins down a "fire line" for the fall harvest

Additional Resources

The Rodale Institute's *Farming for Credit Directory* (www.rodaleinstitute.org/ffc_directory), organized by region, state, and institution, lists sustainable agriculture education opportunities. Each entry includes the name of the farm or program, pertinent websites, and details such as year founded, acres in cultivation, primary outlets for the harvest, and available academic credits and certificates.

For related information, as well as listings of international courses and degree programs, and on-the-job, non-academic learning opportunities in sustainable and organic agriculture, see the USDA's *Educational and Training Opportunities in Sustainable Agriculture*, available online through the Alternative Farming Systems Information Center (http://afsic.nal.usda.gov), and the National Center for Appropriate Technology's directory of *Sustainable Farming Internships and Apprenticeships* (http://attra.ncat.org/attra-pub/internships).

« **Braiding and hanging onions in the storage loft of the barn**

GROWING
A GARDEN
CITY

A PLACE FOR NEIGHBORS TO GATHER. A SHARED *work site and source of sustenance. A place of beauty. A place for self-reliance. Somewhere to play, to ponder, to exercise, and to enjoy. These requisites for an ideal community can all be fulfilled by a single community garden.*

The Family:

Gita Saedi Kiely and Jason Kiely

2nd Street Community Garden Members

"Once you learn that you can feed yourself, you find other ways to feed yourself more of what you need. For us, this garden was the foundation for trying to go as local as possible."

Gita Saedi Kiely is a documentary filmmaker and adjunct faculty member at the University of Montana School of Journalism. Her films include *The New Americans*, a three-part, seven-hour PBS series following five immigrant families to and in the United States. Jason Kiely is a former community organizer for labor and environmental groups. He now serves as director of marketing for Rivertop Renewables, a chemical products startup founded by his father.

The couple met and married in Chicago before moving in 2003 to Missoula, where much of Jason's family lives. Their son Cyrus was born in 2005 and their daughter Soraya two years later.

GITA: We moved in about four years ago—Jason and I and my pregnant belly. We needed a bigger place because we were having this child, but we couldn't really afford a house and a yard. So we found this house without a yard, but we had an adjacent weed-infested dirt lot just staring at us in the face. It was forgotten city land.

JASON: If you look at the map of Missoula, this is the new center of the population. It's next to the Good Food Store and close to the river trail. There's the Sawmill District being developed where there used to be a sawmill and a refinery. In the neighborhood, there are a lot of multi-units, some mobile homes, a lot of older homes, a couple landmarks, and at least six new mid-range family homes like ours. There's a new affordable housing development. Down the street are higher-end condos. Neighbors either have small lots or rent and don't have access to any kind of land.

GITA: That was a big rationale behind the garden.

JASON: We had a child on the way, so we were going to be home anyway and available during the summer to get the garden going.

GITA: We really wanted to make it happen. I come from the Chicago suburbs and we were in the city for a long time before we moved to Missoula. Maybe it's something that happens in middle age, but I'd been wanting so much to garden. It was a yearning that I had when we first moved to Missoula and it grew when we moved into this house.

JASON: The whole idea was, okay, let's get this city lot irrigated, de-weeded, and turned up enough to measure out plots and grow some food.

GITA: We talked to [Community Gardens Director] Tim Hall at Garden City Harvest and he agreed that this would be a great spot for a garden if the neighborhood was going to support it.

JASON: Interest in the neighborhood was easy to measure. I literally went door to door in a three-by-four-block area and asked folks if they would be interested. My goal was, one, to gauge general community support and, two, to identify possible opposition.

I started with the immediate neighbors, and they were all supportive of the idea. There was a recognition that, yeah, this neighborhood actually could use a community garden. I collected names, phone numbers, and e-mail addresses, and there were about fifty folks, with a good twelve to fifteen who seemed significantly interested. I was doing this in October into November, my deadline being a grant from the Missoula Neighborhood Projects Fund. Then, because we were in an Urban Renewal District for which there was a pot of money to do infrastructure improvements, we made the case to the Missoula Redevelopment Agency that bringing the water line out to the garden was a public good. Getting those grants—a total of about $7,000—gave real legitimacy to the idea.

GITA: We got the money in the winter and we started excavating and got the water in before the spring. Then we held work days and got volunteers set up throughout the spring and summer. It took a whole season for us to get everybody involved.

JASON: Tim Hall drove over a sod-busting device and tore up the dirt. He had a volunteer over here shaking out the clods. Montana Conservation Corps donated a day of their youth camp to dig a trench to bury our water line. We had a couple of organized days when neighbors would help. This is lake bed, so there are plenty of rocks, and we made a group decision that there had to be a tall fence because deer roam the area. We rented one of those two-person augers and Tim and I got beat up by that for a couple days. These augers, they don't really dig in ground like this; they loosened the ground and then somebody else was there with the spud bar, pulling out rocks. We sunk our post holes in concrete and used different levels to get them straight. The twelve-year-old son of one of the gardeners was the concrete mixer.

GITA: There was a core of people in this eclectic neighborhood who wanted to garden and make it happen. Single moms with kids in Fireweed Court got involved. People from the multi-units got involved. Folks from the trailers. A botanist who lives in one of the apartments. Bruce, who ran the "Impeach Bush" group in town and sings in a choir. The first year was very collective. We didn't have individual plots. We just planted whatever people offered. Everything was donated either from Garden City Harvest or one of the nurseries in town.

JASON: People found their specific roles. For instance, our next-door neighbor Terry had a lot going on that summer and she wasn't up for gardening, but she likes projects, so she became—what did she call herself—the Queen of Compost?

GITA: The Commander of Compost.

JASON: She took on getting the compost going that first year.

GITA: There was just no way that we would ever have become this cohesive gang without the garden. Getting together, we got to know each other and got to know the neighborhood.

JASON: The neighbors that we talk to the most and see the most, Bruce—

GITA: He's always bragging about his squash.

JASON: Bruce does starts in his kitchen starting in March. He's all over it. In a lot of ways he's the most prolific gardener. I bet Bruce practically eats exclusively from his garden during the summer other than buying meats and grains elsewhere. The most scientifically geared one is John the botanist. He always has some cool heirloom varieties he picks up here and there and does really well with, and he's taken on a native plant project around the edges of the fence. Then there's Ali, a new gardener who really worked hard this year and got a lot out of her garden. The night that Cyrus and I were out trying to get in the last of the tomatoes before the hard freeze she was here doing the same thing. There's a single dad, Jacob, right next to our plot, who's got a total green thumb. Often when we're out there in the summer watering or harvesting in the evening, Terry, she's out on her back porch reading a book or just comes out to talk to us.

GITA: Some gardeners last year taught us about square foot grid gardening. As we looked at other plots, theirs always had the most variety and it was the prettiest and the most interesting. These folks ended up leaving the state, but they were very good at square foot gardening, so we wanted to mimic their success. We did a ton of prep and we created these six beds specifically shaped so that we could square foot garden within them.

JASON: We grew a couple different kinds of tomatoes this year. Spinach.

GITA: Lots of lettuces. Beans, snap peas.

JASON: Our beets did well this year. Carrots did well. Broccoli did phenomenal on either end of the season, which kind of surprised us just because we thought it was done. It went to seed in the summer, but it came back strong in the fall.

GITA: A couple types of squash. Both purple and green peppers. Hot peppers. Mint, curly and Italian parsley, basil, rosemary. And lavender and some flowers.

JASON: Garden City Harvest has an opening day in April. They invite the gardeners from the previous year to come back and claim their plots at ten o'clock and then at noon they invite new gardeners to come and get what's left and sign

up on a first-come, first-serve basis. This year, there was enough interest to plow up another plot or two.

GITA: It feeds on itself. We've been working on this garden for a few years and now Jason is hunting and we just bought a local quarter of a cow. Once you learn that you can feed yourself, you find other ways to feed yourself more of what you need.

For us, this garden was the foundation for trying to go as local as possible. I absolutely do not have green thumbs, but as we're becoming smarter gardeners, we have quite a variety of vegetables. I made a pasta sauce with the leftover tomatoes. I make stews in the slow cooker with all of our vegetables and the cow from our deep freeze, and it's so satisfying to make this meal that we're going to eat for three days. That satisfaction that comes from really creating and participating in what we eat surprised me. Like tonight we ate a vegetable soup that was all from our garden: carrots, squash, eggplants, a beet, onion, and a lot of herbs. I basically roasted everything and pureed it and added coconut milk. It tasted really good! I threw in roasted mint and the soup tasted a little Persian—it tasted like *aush*—which is really funny because we made it in Missoula, Montana. Because of the roasted mint it was accidentally a lot like a soup my mom would have made.

JASON: Last year, during the second season, we had a baby girl, so now we have a three-year-old and a one-year-old. I can just put the baby down in the backyard and jump the fence to get tomatoes for dinner. In Chicago "local" was sixty miles away. Here it's right next door.

**ANY ONE
COMMUNITY GARDEN
CAN BENEFIT A**
*particular neighborhood
and its residents. A
network of gardens can
transform an entire
city's sense of self.*

The Organizer:

Tim Hall

Community Gardens Director

"It takes three years to turn a patch of dirt into something that looks like, 'Hey now, that's something going on over there.' It takes five years for it to look really good. And at ten years it's a damned oasis and we think, 'Why didn't we do that sooner?'"

Tim Hall walks half a block from the used sporting goods store he co-owns, the Sports Exchange, to be interviewed after work. The chosen rendez-vous, a café, is jammed and noisy, but he exudes calm. If real trouble arises, he can always handle it with his tractor.

Garden City Harvest operates seven community gardens. The cost of a 15' x 15' plot is $35 for the season plus a $15 clean-up deposit. Included are water, tools, compost, and advice.

One or two generations ago my family were all farmers. It wasn't something my dad did, but my great-uncle and my grandfather and great-grandfather were farmers, and I have distinct memories as a young guy of being around farms. I always had this respect for where my food came from. Even as a college kid, thinking a lot—I was the first kid in my family to go to a four-year university—I always thought, as an environmentalist, I shouldn't criticize somebody if I haven't seen life through their lens.

From an ecology and environmental studies background in college, I landed my first job as a land use planner working for a county government in northern New York. Long story short, I did that for about two years, in which time my father passed away, so I stayed at my job and made sure that my mom and my brothers and our family unit were back together, and then I put it all behind me. I was doing environmental work and it was important, but working in a bureaucracy wasn't really what I wanted to do.

I had always had a pang to go west, so I moved west and I lived on this ranch in Oregon, on an island in the middle of a tidal coastal river. We had eleven-foot tides. It was a phenomenal experience, living by and understanding the rhythms of the place. I worked with animals for the first time. We had cows, we had sheep, we had every sort of fowl and chicken and goose that could be, and we birthed them, we pulled them, we kept them alive, and we had to put a few down. We got into that whole cycle of connection to place and to food and it wasn't always pretty. I learned how to run a tractor and farm and fence, solving problems as they came up, being able to prioritize situations and do a lot with a little in that pioneer spirit. The other thing I learned was that work didn't stop when five o'clock came. It started when it started and it ended when it ended. Some days were long and some days were short. That was part of life and that was part of farming.

When I left New York I had said I would never be a planner again, but I actually left the ranch for a job in Missoula, working on regional planning and engaging people in conversation about their sense of place and how to preserve it. As part of that, I was connected to the working farms and ranches in the county, and one day Josh Slotnick and Caitlin DeSilvey came to my office and asked me about gleaning apples at Fort Missoula. They were just beginning Garden City Harvest and they had this sort of think tank, and I tried my best as a government employee to find them land and to provide counsel. Ultimately, I ended up being the chairman of this loose group of advisors. When the position of community gardens director opened, I applied and became a staff member.

At the time we had three gardens: the North Side Garden, which we inherited from the Missoula Urban Demonstration Project; the River Road Garden, which was the original piece of land Josh and Kim rented when they moved to Missoula; and the ASUM Garden, which had been founded by the University of Montana Garden Club. These were run by volunteers, people who had a passion and maybe gardened there and didn't get any pay, but made sure the thing

ran. Where it got a little shaky was that there were some eighty plots to manage, and when equipment was bought, things would get stolen. So the first thing I instituted was hiring a paid coordinator.

This go-to person is the key in all these gardens for success. You rent your plot, you pay your fee, and the organizer is there to make sure that the basic rules are being followed, things are safe, the tools and supplies are there, the needs are being met, and the water is on. Once the season is up and going, I check in with all my garden organizers once a week to make sure that they have the resources they need to make their little gardens function and that they're interacting with the gardeners. Gardening can be intimidating and we want to make sure that we have an inviting place where the gardeners know they can go to the organizer with questions. All my garden organizers are very passionate about place. Some of them may not be the best gardeners, but after a season they're a hell of a lot better than they were, and they're very capable teachers.

Every spring we start rough and I see all these different places, each with its own personality, its own leaders, its own issues, get better and better. A school garden at Meadow Hill School was started because the after-school program coordinator contacted me and said, "I think we'd like to do this." We went over there and I tore that place up with a tractor. [Laughs] This was a dirt heap with knapweed stalks sticking out of it—I wasn't even sure if it would grow food—but we tore it up, we got the weeds out as best we could, we brought in soil amendments, we brought in topsoil, we put compost down, we brought in manure, and three years later it looks good. Success at that school led us this year to a new Willard School garden. We started a garden on 2nd Street on a leftover, almost-abandoned piece of city property. With neighborhood spunk and spirit and a little bit of guidance from us and money from the city, it's been turned into a place where people are growing their own food, and it's only going to get better.

It takes three years to turn a patch of dirt into something that looks like, "Hey now, that's something going on over there." It takes five years for it to look really good. And at ten years it's a damned oasis and we think, "Why didn't we do that sooner?" You have to have a vision. You have to see the potential. I'm always telling people, "You know, three years from now this is going to look great."

At the gardens, neighbors meet, and rich and poor interact. Our surveys indicate that many people who garden have adequate income to buy their food elsewhere or buy a CSA share. Some even have their own gardens at home. But they choose to garden at the community garden for other reasons. Maybe they like that it's a really good deal—$35 buys you an entire season of water, compost, soil, and straw—but I think community is a big part of it. Meeting people in adjacent parcels. Talking, teaching, learning. If my plot is 52B and yours is 52A, by the end of the season you and I probably know each other pretty well. Maybe I've even given you some vegetables and you watered when I was on vacation.

People helping each other out is our magic. We're always cultivating volunteer groups and individuals, building bridges, and making sure our program is available to all people. Our edible open spaces are safe and near people, where they can grow their own food, where they can teach their children about where food comes from, where they can touch the soil. It's the fullest sense of community and I make sure we're coordinating with the neighborhoods we're serving and that the food we're growing is going to people who need it—either in exchange for their volunteerism or by being distributed to the food bank, the Poverello Center [soup kitchen], or some of our other non-profit partners. When youth home summer staff were looking for activities to do with their children, we invited them to volunteer. Not everybody knows how to do everything, but you get ten young people to come over as a group and they can do stellar work. Whether individuals or organizations volunteer to grow the food or to take the food, they're helping us support our mission.

My phone always rings. Every week I get a call from somebody who's conjuring up a new garden. "What does it take?" "How do you set up your water?" "How big are your plots?" "What works?" I'm getting calls from Great Falls, Bozeman, Helena, Livingston, Coeur d'Alene, Salt Lake City. I got a call from Duke University two days

TIM HALL

73

ago. [Laughs] I'm like, "What are you guys doing calling *me*?" But we have something that's working.

I try to make them think that it's possible. I help people find access to places to grow their own food, and I share with them that it's not rocket science; anyone can do this. The first couple of years are going to be rough—if you build it, they may not come—but by year two, three, four, or five, everybody will want a plot. What's critical to success those first few years is having the vision, the chutzpah, the where-withal to rally your experienced veterans and people who don't know anything but have the energy.

We're about to do it again next spring at a site by the Joseph Residence, which is transitional housing for sixteen different homeless families. The Catholic Church has an acre and a half of land next to a ditch, and parish members knew me and were into local food. Well, we had a meeting to see if we could put together a garden there that wouldn't benefit just the Joseph Residence and the church, but the greater neighborhood. There's a social justice factor to helping others who can't grow food or don't have a place to do it, and to distributing food to those people. The week before Halloween, out of nowhere, you drive up in a van and bring pumpkins to young people whose moms and dads can't afford them, and it blows their minds. Going to the food bank and seeing people come out of there with local food, that's why we do the work we do, that feels good, that keeps me going.

The need for more gardens has heightened. In collaboration with homeWORD, a nonprofit here in Missoula, we started Orchard Gardens to link affordable housing with a small neighborhood farm and community garden, and I'm excited about some new and old relationships that are being kindled with parks departments because neighbors are contacting those organizations about having gardens. We've got these public lands—we can use them at least in part for outdoor classrooms, for summer gardens, for places where people in the neighborhood can get together safely and maybe beautify their community. This is a win-win all the way around. If we can help, mission accomplished. In twenty years I think there should and will be gardens on every little patch of nothing that's out there.

How It Works

Community Gardens

Neighborhood-based community gardens provide many benefits to local residents, including household garden plots, access to tools and advice, and beautiful, peaceful places where families and neighbors gather to enjoy growing healthy, delicious food.

Background

Community gardens are working vibrant green spaces, developed and shared by neighborhood residents and the public, promoting gardeners as project "owners" and leaders. Because community gardeners make more use of gardens in their immediate vicinity, Garden City Harvest prefers locations in low-income neighborhoods where their benefits are needed most. Here families without yard space or gardening experience can rent a small plot to grow vegetables and meet their own desire for fresh, healthy food.

The Gardens

Garden City Harvest operates more than half a dozen community gardens, each designed to suit a specific neighborhood or constituency in need. Cost per plot is $35 for the season plus a $15 clean-up deposit, with space awarded on a first-come, first-serve basis. On an opening day in mid-April, veteran gardeners come early to reserve their plots, followed by new gardeners.

These gardens include:

- ASUM Community Garden: Located behind university student housing and supported in part by the University of Montana student government, this site serves mainly student gardeners, who receive preference for plots.
- Meadow Hill School and Community Garden: Located on the grounds of a middle school, this site offers plots for lease to community members in addition to garden space reserved for use by multiple school and after-school programs.
- Orchard Gardens Community Garden and Neighborhood Farm: This garden is located at the center of an affordable housing development whose residents receive preference for plots. Attached is a small farm further serving the local low-income population with a subsidized CSA, farm stand, and produce for the Missoula Food Bank and Youth Harvest Mobile Market. Through a popular "volunteers for veggies" program, participants can earn free produce in exchange for their labor.
- North Side Community Garden: This busy, well-established, seventy-plot garden has served local residents of a mixed-income neighborhood for three decades.
- River Road Community Garden and Neighborhood Farm: This site combines garden plots for lease and two CSA programs, with additional food grown to give to area youth homes and the Poverello Center soup kitchen. As at Orchard Gardens, the farm needs and rewards "volunteers for veggies" participants for its operation.

« Gathering water

- 2nd Street Garden: This recently established garden on a former vacant city lot serves a changing neighborhood near the center of town, and was developed in partnership with municipal funds for urban redevelopment and renewal.
- Garden of Eaton: Garden City Harvest's newest site (located on Eaton Street) is a collaboration with a transitional housing center for homeless families and a local Catholic church. Plots serve members of the neighborhood, the parish that donated the land, and occupants of the transitional residence.

Recipe for Success

The basic ingredients of a successful community garden are on-site tools, water for irrigation, and community spaces such as herb and flower gardens, children's gardens, picnic tables, shady spots, and play areas. "All our sites are kid-friendly and good family places," says Tim Hall, community gardens director.

Written rules and guidelines address such concerns as abandoned plots, weeds, and parking or watering restrictions, overseen by a designated garden organizer. At Garden City Harvest, organizers are paid part-time employees. Garden plot holders rely on them to ensure that rules are being followed and necessary tools and supplies are available, and to answer any questions.

Planning a new garden starts with neighborhood involvement. "There was a core of people in this eclectic neighborhood who wanted to garden and make this happen," says Gita Saedi Kiely, a founding member of the 2nd Street Community Garden. "Single moms with kids . . . people from the multi-units . . . folks from the trailers . . . a botanist who lives in one of the apartments." Her husband Jason Kiely collected contact information for fifty approving residents.

Next seek grants, sponsors, and volunteers, if possible. Because the 2nd Street Community Garden was in an Urban Renewal District, for example, the site received public funding for its water

Early summer community garden plots »

THE URBAN GARDEN

line connection. Tim Hall recalls another garden built in large part by members of a church group service project. "There were young people and old people and they found out about us through another member of the Missoula community," Hall says. "For four days we got to put them to work doing daunting projects, and at the end of it they thanked us and they meant it. They appreciated the work that we were doing, and we showed them a good time."

Patience, persistence, and participation seal the deal. Veteran gardeners count on enthusiastic newcomers, and vice-versa. Fertile, great-looking grounds may take years to develop, but once they do, says Hall, "everybody will want a plot."

Additional Resources

The American Community Gardening Association facilitates the formation and expansion of state and regional community gardening networks, develops resources in support of community gardening,

« **Weeding together**

and conducts related research and educational programs. Their website (www
.communitygarden.org) hosts a bookstore, *Ten Steps to Starting a Community Garden*
tipsheet, and national community garden database, e-newsletter, and list-serv.

Books for garden organizers and community gardeners include *Brooklyn Botanic
Garden All-Region Guides: Community Gardening,* edited by Ellen Kirby and Eliza-
beth Peters; *Burpee Complete Gardener: A Comprehensive, Up-to-Date, Fully Illus-
trated Reference for Gardeners at All Levels* by Allan Armitage, Maureen Heffernan,
Chela Kleiber, and Holly H. Shimizu; and *Organic Gardening for Dummies* by Ann
Whitman and the editors of the National Gardening Association.

The USDA Master Gardener Program offers free or low-cost person-to-person
gardening tips and training in all fifty states and the District of Columbia. To find local
programs listed by state or Canadian province, consult the Cooperative Extension
Service website (www.extension.org/pages/extension_master_gardener).

See Also

« Taking home the harvest

A VIBRANT COMMUNITY ADAPTS WITH THE SEASONS *yet never goes dormant. Eating locally is possible even in a harsh climate, be it that of the Arizona desert, the Alaskan tundra, or under the ever-variable Montana sky.*

The Foodie:

Jodi Allison-Bunnell

River Road Neighborhood Farm
CSA Member

"One fundamental fact of a CSA and of seasonal eating is that you have to accept that you are not in charge of the food. It is, in fact, in charge of you."

LOCAVORES FOR PEACE, reads the hand-lettered sign in Jodi Allison-Bunnell's first-floor window. An archivist by profession, she manages the digital archives program of the Orbis Cascade Alliance, a consortium of three dozen academic libraries. Her husband Steve is an educational software developer. Their son Camas is eight.

My background was the conventional, middle-American diet. Food was obtained mostly from the grocery store, and my childhood friends and I ate macaroni and cheese and Pop Tarts. This was before farmers' markets were widely available, but my family would go out to the orchards, and I was always very conscious that we needed to support local farmers in order to keep them on the land. So when Steve and I were first married, in the early and mid-nineties, living in an apartment in Washington, D.C., we found all the U-pick farms around D.C. and went out and picked berries and cherries and peaches and apples. When we came to Missoula it was just natural to keep doing those things, to seek out apples, to visit the farmers' market. Somewhere along the line, at the farmers' market, somebody at the Garden City Harvest stand handed us free kale, and said, "Don't you want to sign up for a CSA?" And we said [confused], "Sure. . . ."

It became quickly evident to us that a CSA was a few-hundred-dollar subscription you bought at the beginning of the season, and then you got a share of the harvest throughout the summer. Here we have a sixteen-to-eighteen-week growing season, and once a week we picked up our share of vegetables at the garden. This started off in June, with salad greens, spinach, and bok choy, and lasted right up to the pumpkins, the first or second week of October. I thought it was wonderful. I hated that typical home-economics scenario where, as the budget-minded housewife, you plan your meals out at the beginning of the week, and then you make your shopping list, and you go out shopping. With a CSA, it's all about working with what's available. All you can do is say, "Look, squash, cabbage, kale—what can we make today?"

Gradually a much more expanded form of eating local food crept up on us. After we got a CSA, our naturopath advised us to eat more lamb. We discovered that, of course, lamb was very expensive in the store, so we started working with meat producers directly to buy whole lambs. We found local chickens raised by this really nice family down in Florence, and more and more people we could get fruit from. Then some neighbors of ours read Gary Paul Nabhan's *Coming Home to Eat* and they called people together with Greg Price, the farmer at River Road, and Tim Hall at Garden City Harvest, and said, "Can we start a winter share program?"

A winter share is designed to feed a family of four their vegetables from October through May. From one source, you're getting all the onions, potatoes, carrots, corn, cucumbers, cauliflower, leeks, beets, broccoli, celery root, squash, green beans, greens, tomatoes, sweet peppers, and hot peppers that can be kept successfully over the winter one way or another, by drying, freezing, canning, or root-cellaring. At that point we were already kind of eating within our region, but bananas and broccoli still appeared in my shopping cart in the middle of winter. I thought, "Why don't we try *really* doing it?" So we were among the first subscribers.

One fundamental fact of a CSA and of seasonal eating is that you have to accept that you are not in charge of the food. It is, in fact, in charge of you. When the food's ready, you have to be ready for it. I mean, here we are, sitting in the living room, and what do we have here? About eighty pounds of squash, all lined up by the heat vents, curing for the winter. Hanging up in the garage now, curing, too, are 150 pounds of onions. The greens we harvested ourselves and froze. Other things like tomatoes came in four or five waves, and the tomatoes don't care if you are out of town or on a deadline for a project or if your kid is sick. [Laughs] At first it's a little like having multiple children show up when you only expected one.

Besides just being ready when all the food comes in, you have to have a certain space and set of skills and equipment in order to deal with it. Steve and his uncle built a root cellar into the end of the furnace room, where it stays about 50 to 55 degrees and the humidity's about 40 percent, and that's where the potatoes and onions and garlic and carrots and beets and celery root go. There's another root cellar that came with the house built into the vault under the front steps and that's where the fruit goes because the ethylene gas that comes off the fruit will make the potatoes sprout if they're together. Along with a cool basement, we have two freezers and we know all the blanching times for freezing vegetables. Canning is chemistry in action and you really do need to know how acidic the vegetables are and whether you need

to acidify them, and that's knowledge we've acquired. So far this year, from the CSA, we've canned pickles, relishes, tomato quarters, tomato juice, ketchup, spaghetti sauce, and salsa; dried sweet peppers for chili; root-cellared onions, garlic, three kinds of potatoes, and six kinds of squash; and frozen kale, mustard greens, broccoli, collards, cauliflower, green beans, and corn.

When people ask me about it, they comment, "Well, this must take just a god-awful amount of time." And in some ways it does, but really, when it's February and it's time to make dinner, what I have on hand are half-prepared foods. So if I'm making a quick spaghetti dinner, I thaw out some bison and make meatballs, grab a jar of canned spaghetti sauce, cook pasta, and have what we call winter salad, which is steamed kale with salad dressing on it. There's dinner. It's the quintessential women's magazine twenty-to-thirty-minute preparation time.

It's harder this way to eat badly. We eat a lot more vegetables than the average American because that's what we have. We both work from home, so lunch is usually leftovers from last night's dinner for all three of us—my son takes it to school in a thermos—and, you know, greens and eggs are not unheard of on our breakfast menu. So sometimes we have vegetables three times a day. I think it gives us a pretty broad diet. We have a seven-year-old who will eat almost anything. He is wildly enthusiastic when I tell him we're having steamed kale with salad dressing. He thinks that's just the greatest thing. And I think that's pretty great, too. Here we are in the middle of the city. We're not homesteaders. We're not back-to-the-landers. We're fitting this in with our family life and careers. This is not back to the ways of our great-grandparents because they had to grow it all themselves. Greg always emphasizes how much he learns from the land, but the amount of knowledge and skill that goes into organic farming the way he does, planting and harvesting with volunteer labor, and running a CSA business is amazing.

I was curious, as we tried to make a reasonable effort to eat locally, where our food dollars would go, so I kept detailed records over five years ending this June of where we spent our money. Every time food came in the house, I would sit

down really quickly with a highlighter and just mark on the receipt what was local. Over five years I found two things. One was that we spent 55 percent of our food dollars locally. The other was that we were not only eating extremely well—our meals included things like nice local chickens and legs of lamb and wine—but we were eating for less than the USDA "moderate" budget plan for a family of our size and composition. The average "moderate" budget for all three family members over this time was about $133 a week, and over those five years we averaged about $120 a week. So there's no real reason that you can't eat locally in Montana. Yeah, the growing season's short, but this is not Siberia. You can even do it in Alaska. I have a friend in Fairbanks who's part of a CSA there, and she reports that it's a very short but very abundant season.

Ten years into doing this in various forms, I can't really imagine doing without it. My son Camas was two when we started going up to River Road, so he's utterly at home there and he doesn't remember eating any other way. Greg is an important part of his life and Greg's chickens are an important part. [Laughs] Camas is one of the designated chicken chasers. The chickens are not supposed to get in certain parts of the garden because they do damage and he's authorized to chase the chickens, which he thinks is great fun. He loves to gather eggs.

Conversations happen when you go out to the garden, either just to pick up a share or, especially, if you go to volunteer. Kids from youth court are there on referral to work. Students from the university are there volunteering for vegetables. There are also volunteers from the community because a large portion of the food is going to the food bank or the homeless shelter. A couple years ago there was a woman out there who was spending her last living days volunteering at River Road. She knew she was sick and this was her choice. She died that fall and I didn't know until I read her obituary that she was a program officer for the National Endowment for the Arts. She talked about all kinds of other things over the rows.

This summer I went to my twentieth high school class reunion and I think a couple people I talked to were at least a little surprised that people with our level of education—my husband has a PhD and I have two master's—spend our time this way. And standing in the kitchen for the umpteen-millionth time blanching greens, there are moments when I think, "Why am I doing this?" But at this point buying fruits and vegetables at the Good Food Store in February seems crazy. When those local Dixon melons come on at the end of the summer, that is a taste absolutely worth waiting for, that's part of where we live. In places like Italy or France they talk about the taste of the land coming through the wine. Well, the taste of the land is also there in your potatoes. You just have to pay attention.

THERE ARE SOME 20,000 COMMUNITY SUPPORTED FARMS *and community gardens in the United States and Canada, and probably as many different paths to become a farm manager or garden organizer. Necessary skills include: sales and bookkeeping, curriculum development and classroom management, equipment maintenance, and the ability to protect unpicked tomatoes from sudden hailstorms. Patience with "helpers" who trample freshly planted cucumbers is a plus.*

The Farmer:

Greg Price

River Road Community Garden and Neighborhood Farm Manager

"I used to wake up in the middle of the night. 'Oh no, I forgot to check on carrot germination and it's day fifteen!' What I've learned over the years lets me sleep."

When he moved across the country after military service and college, Greg Price never meant to lead or serve humankind. "I came to Montana seeking to connect with something other than the people world."

My parents split up when I was young and I grew up in a lot of different places—Baltimore, Maryland; Lancaster, Pennsylvania; Texas—but they were all either suburbia or urban settings. When you're a kid your perspective is about as big as a pea. As a teenager, I believed, emotionally, that I was never going to get out of high school sometimes. After high school, I spent a year working, then went into the military. All of a sudden I was nineteen and living in Germany. I became a junior meteorologist, which kept me outside, immersed in nature. My world started to open up.

After the military I went to college and studied philosophy. I read *Living the Good Life* by Scott Nearing, who talked about an intense connectivity with nature. He was building stone houses that took seven years to build and digging his own pond when he was ninety-five years old! That summer my partner at the time, Laurie, and I dug and planted a huge garden in our backyard in Pennsylvania.

Next door was a house still occupied by a son of the folks who had originally farmed it, and one day he showed us a 1948 picture from the perspective of where we were standing. In this picture there was nothing—the closest neighbor was seven miles away. Now, though, we were on an island of about four houses. Beyond that were two highways and a main road and an auto dealer. When we looked out all we saw was industrial craziness: smoke stacks, pavement, and bridges. I started making connections as to where it led. As humans, we made up our own rules. We made up civilizations not necessarily grounded in anything in the natural world, and, in many ways, we continued to stray further and further away from nature. My interest in food escalated.

The next year Laurie and I took a seven-week trip around the country. We started in Pennsylvania; went down to the south and the southwest; up to California, Oregon, and Idaho; and then, week five, into Montana. On a gloriously sunny day in July we drove into Missoula after backpacking in the Sawtooths. After breakfast, walking around town, we were talking about the place and how we felt when one of us threw it out there: "We should move here." The next thing we know, we're loading up the U-Haul.

We found a house. Laurie found a teaching job. Everything just went beautifully. I had played percussion in a band back in Pennsylvania and I met Josh Slotnick's wife Kim through a drum and dance troupe. I knew they farmed and I asked if I could volunteer with them in exchange for food and knowledge. They said okay, so I did it that summer. The next year Laurie and I bought a house and planted a huge garden and I continued my internship with Kim. Garden City Harvest was just getting started, and, at the end of that second summer, the woman running a food bank garden quit. That was my beginning.

I ran that garden for three years on a very limited piece of ground just above where the PEAS Farm is now and built up a really nice CSA. I had no plan; I had never done anything that big. It was all volunteers, and we were on a *really* low budget. Working twenty to twenty-five hours a week, getting paid for fifteen, I was hand-unloading manure by myself out of pickup trucks in the middle of the night with a headlamp on. I had this old

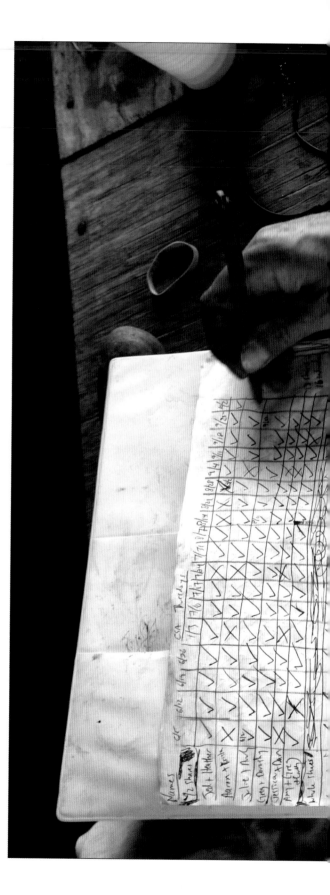

white Jeep I'd pull up ten feet through my field, unload some manure, pull it up ten more feet, unload more manure. We didn't have manure spreaders then. [Laughs] We had one tractor that was way out at Fort Missoula, which took a mighty act to get across town.

When the PEAS Farm moved, my garden's necessity went away, so I took a year off, doing grizzly bear DNA work for a mix of environmental groups from Idaho and Montana, still connecting with nature. I was out in the woods five days out of every seven or eight. Then Clare Emery and Jodi Allison-Bunnell and Mark and Bridget Wilson approached me and Garden City Harvest. They said, "We're trying to figure out how much food we can eat locally year-round. We want to know if you guys are interested in trying to grow a winter CSA." I said I would love to do that. I was very interested in the whole storage aspect of keeping food for the winter. That's how I got to River Road.

There are three major aspects here. We've got forty-two community garden plots on less than an acre, a one-acre farm with summer and winter CSAs and food bank donations, and a program called "volunteer for veggies" where people provide labor in exchange for food. The big wild card is how many people show up to volunteer. A typical CSA day might begin with the youth home kids showing up. I divide them into groups and list the things that have to be harvested that morning. They start and all of a sudden there are two more volunteers, then two more, and then six more. Now I've got twenty people in the garden, and I'm not doing any gardening; I'm just walking around making sure everybody is doing the right thing and answering questions. One group of kids harvests kale, one group digs carrots, another group pulls green onions. Two volunteers pick peas and another two pick beets. When six more people show up, I'll say, "Okay, that's enough people harvesting. You guys are going to go weed the broccoli patch."

Because I want people to show up, I'm very generous with volunteers. If somebody comes and weeds for two hours they're probably going to go home with at least ten pounds of food—for example, two pounds of broccoli, two pounds of carrots, some leaves of kale, a couple onions, a sack full of potatoes, and two or three pounds of tomatoes. That's a surprise to a lot of people. Volunteering for me beats minimum wage.

Of course I have to deal with limited skill sets. People come in with the view that this is monkey work—there's nothing to it. But when somebody plants fifty feet of broccoli and I tell them that they have to redo the whole thing, they look at me like I'm crazy. I have them stand up and I say, "Look at the rows. They don't have to be maniacally straight, but they can't go from eight inches apart to twenty inches apart."

This farm produces roughly 30,000 pounds of food on an acre. When people discover the world of details involved in doing that, their eyes open wide. Say there's some flea beetles on the potatoes—I need to take care of those. Is it windy? Then I need to spray at dusk so that the spray stays on and is effective. If the carrots need to be thinned, we probably have a week to get to that until they get out of control. We might still have some late planting to do, so I need to plant beans today. Maybe I need to check the germination on the corn. Depending on what day it is, I've got to move the water.

Each year I get a little better. I started the winter CSA with eight or ten members and I think they paid $250 for 500 pounds of local organic food. [Laughs] That was an obscene steal for them. It took me three years to grow good broccoli. It took me four years to learn when corn was absolutely ripe. For years, I put in an extraordinary amount of physical effort and studying. In general, organic farming is more about creating good soil than it is about taking care of your plants. Once you create the right soil base and you rotate properly and you have a good plant variety, the area becomes a healthy ecosystem. I used to wake up in the middle of the night. "Oh no, I forgot to check on carrot germination and it's day fifteen!" What I've learned over the years lets me sleep.

We have thirty summer shares and fifteen winter shares, and demand rises every year. Last year, all shares were sold out by the first week in March—three months

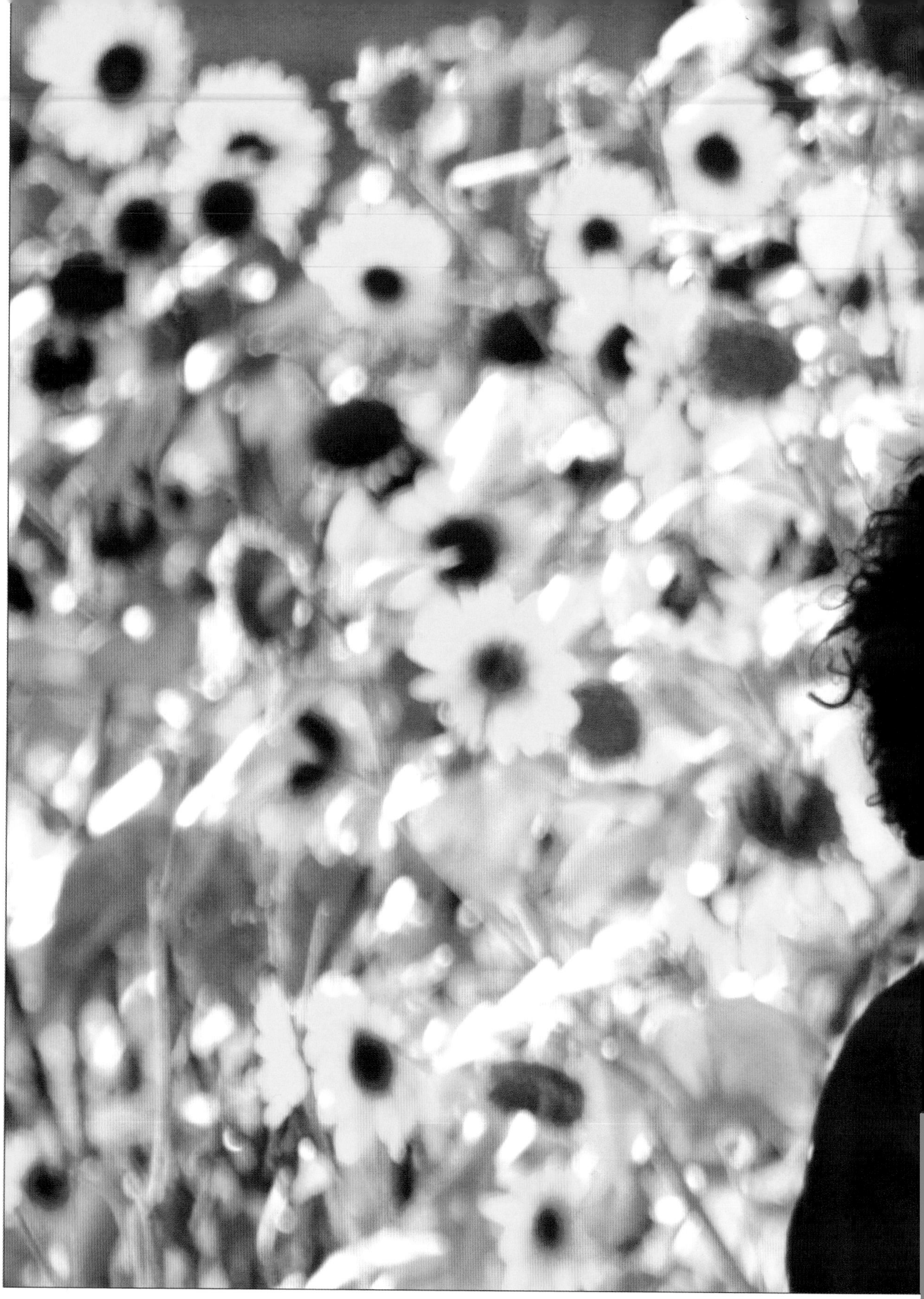

before the first pick up for summer shares. For the first time ever, I have a waiting list for winter shares. There's been the same progression with community garden plots. The first year, out of forty-two plots, there were twenty-five rented; the next year we had thirty-five; for the last four years, it's been sold out with a waiting list. People want two plots, three plots, four if they can have them. That's my value system—storing food and eating as much locally as you can.

There are 3.25 acres total on the property, which includes a house and yard. I take care of all the land, but we occupy only about two acres. On the rest, I expand the vegetable farming a little bit every year, but the other part of expansion is infrastructure, and we haven't dived into that because the land is leased. We're in an urban area that's been intensely in-filled over the last ten years, so the setting is perfect for urban agriculture, but the long-term security of it is fifty-fifty. In Iowa and Ohio, big ag pays $200 an acre. This land is roughly $150,000 to $250,000 an acre—housing development prices—a half million to a million dollars for the whole property. As an organization, we're making an effort to secure the land, but can we really pay that price to farm?

Of course, emotionally for me, there is no price. I'm a pretty pragmatic person, but for me community isn't sitting in a movie theater, it's not sitting in a restaurant, it's not even being at a political rally. People have to interact with each other. There are over 300 people directly involved with this site. From all different aspects of our culture they interact under a value system of caring for a piece of land, getting their food from it, and letting nature work in and around it. You can read *The Omnivore's Dilemma* all day long, but you're not going to fully get what community means unless you get out and participate. You've got to have hands-on experience to gain that appreciation.

Satisfaction comes when I see other people make the connection. It may be the youth home kids realizing where food comes from. At the end of the year they look me in the eye and say "Thanks" and I know that they got something from me. It may be a volunteer that one day sits down and says, "Man, I had no idea. This kale is incredible. After that kale and egg breakfast that you told me to eat I feel like Superman." Likewise, I've had that same experience without people—with the ground, with insects, with birds, foxes, skunks, and deer, with the soft cartoonish light in September setting over the garden, and the vibrancy of flowers, with all these beautiful plants growing nutrition for our community.

Farming, in general, is hard physical labor. There's a little more romanticism about it than I can tolerate at times. Because if it were so romantic then where is everybody wanting to farm? Day in, day out, it's a rhythm of very hard work, punctuated by profoundly romantic moments. But I sit quietly and I think about some of those things when I'm in the garden. Sometimes at night I just sit by myself and listen.

How It Works

Community Supported Agriculture (CSA)

In community supported agriculture programs, or CSAs, local food systems grow from a direct farmer-consumer connection. Farmers benefit by securing a consistent customer base for their goods. Members, meanwhile, enjoy the freshest, tastiest food possible, often at prices far below those for comparable products at a grocery store. For both parties, an additional reward is the relationship with each other: farmers gain satisfaction in meeting the fellow community members who eat their food, and consumers take pride in knowing their farmer and from where their food comes.

Background

In a CSA, members "subscribe" to a local farm by paying up-front for a regular share of its seasonal harvest. Though available produce changes weekly, the total number of shares is restricted so as to supply a consistent amount of food per customer per week. In the case of Garden City Harvest CSA, for example, each weekly share feeds a typical family of four.

Like the communities they serve, every CSA is unique. Some include a choice of goods, as at a farmers' market. In others, multiple operators combine to offer not only fresh local vegetables, but also fruit, flowers, eggs, bread, meats, cheeses, and other farm products. Pickup may take place at farms themselves, pre-arranged neighborhood drop-off points, or even via home delivery.

As is true of Garden City Harvest CSAs, many community supported agriculture programs offer sliding-scale memberships and grow extra produce for food banks, soup kitchens, youth homes, senior residences, and others in need.

The CSAs

Garden City Harvest operates three CSAs. Each provides fresh, local, organic vegetables and a way for participants to connect to food, farming, and place, but involvement, pricing, and the amount of food provided differ as follows:

- PEAS Farm: PEAS and Youth Harvest students help to grow dozens of varieties of vegetables for an eighty-share CSA throughout the summer and early fall. Cost per share is $500 for approximately 200 pounds of food, with discounts available to low- and moderate-income members. Also available may be weekly flower and egg shares.

  Proceeds fund the growing of tens of thousands of pounds more food for the Missoula Food Bank and Youth Harvest Mobile Market.

- River Road Neighborhood Farm: A program similar to the PEAS Farm CSA, River Road sells thirty summer and fifteen winter CSA shares. Each summer shareholder pays $425 for eighteen weeks of vegetables during the growing season. Participants in the separate winter shares system, meanwhile, pay $450 for roughly 450 pounds of food harvested at the end of the growing season which are ideal for freezing, canning, and storing long into winter and spring. Members of either type may volunteer in the fields to reduce the cost of a share.

Thousands of pounds of food grown at the River Road Neighborhood Farm each year supply local youth homes and the Poverello Center soup kitchen.

- Orchard Gardens Neighborhood Farm: Serving residents of the surrounding affordable housing development and others, the twenty-share Orchard Gardens

⌄ **CSA pick-up day**

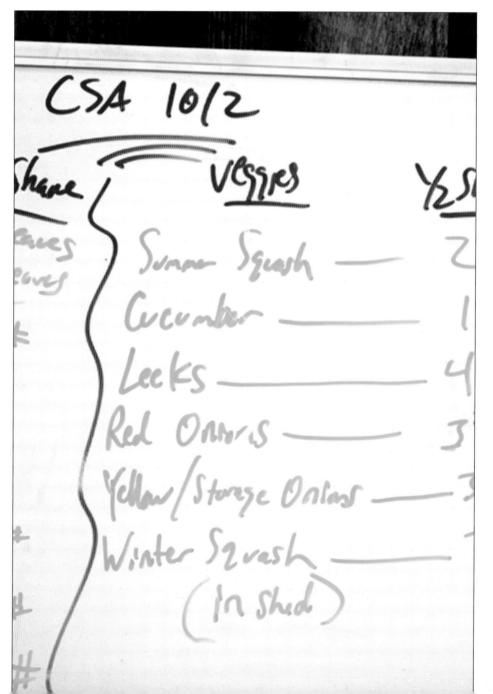

CSA accepts food stamps as well as payment on a sliding scale corresponding to income in exchange for sixteen weeks of vegetables, including greens, tomatoes, carrots, cucumbers, broccoli, potatoes, onions, garlic, and squash.

Additional food grown on-site helps stock a subsidized farm stand, the Missoula Food Bank, and the Youth Harvest Mobile Market.

Be Prepared

Joining a CSA means a fundamental change in shopping, cooking, and eating habits. Ask your farm or farmer what foods to expect, when, and in what quantity, and seek the advice of veteran CSA members about how to store and prepare food, and what else to buy to supplement what's in season. "It's all about working with what's available," says River Road CSA member Jodi Allison-Bunnell. Her family's meals include "nice local chickens and legs of

Organizing the harvest »

lamb and wine," but cost less than the USDA "moderate" budget plan for comparable households.

When cooking, work backward rather than forward from cookbooks, checking what you have, then consulting the index for recipes—or look for local, seasonal cookbooks and other "local eating" guides. "Because I got a lot of cabbage, I made a lot of coleslaw," says Orchard Gardens CSA member Kim Markuson. "I would grab cilantro, garlic, onions, and different kinds of tomatoes, and make fresh salsa and tomato sauce. I made pesto and I'd never made pesto before. I'd never had gnocchi before and we made it from scratch."

In exchange for new habits, expect different but fresher, healthier, and ultimately better-tasting meals.

Additional Resources

The USDA National Agriculture Library supplies government publications about CSAs (online at www.nal .usda.gov/afsic/pubs/csa/csa.shtml), while

Carrots, peppers, and onions awaiting measurement »

Gathering
eggs for
members
of an egg
share »

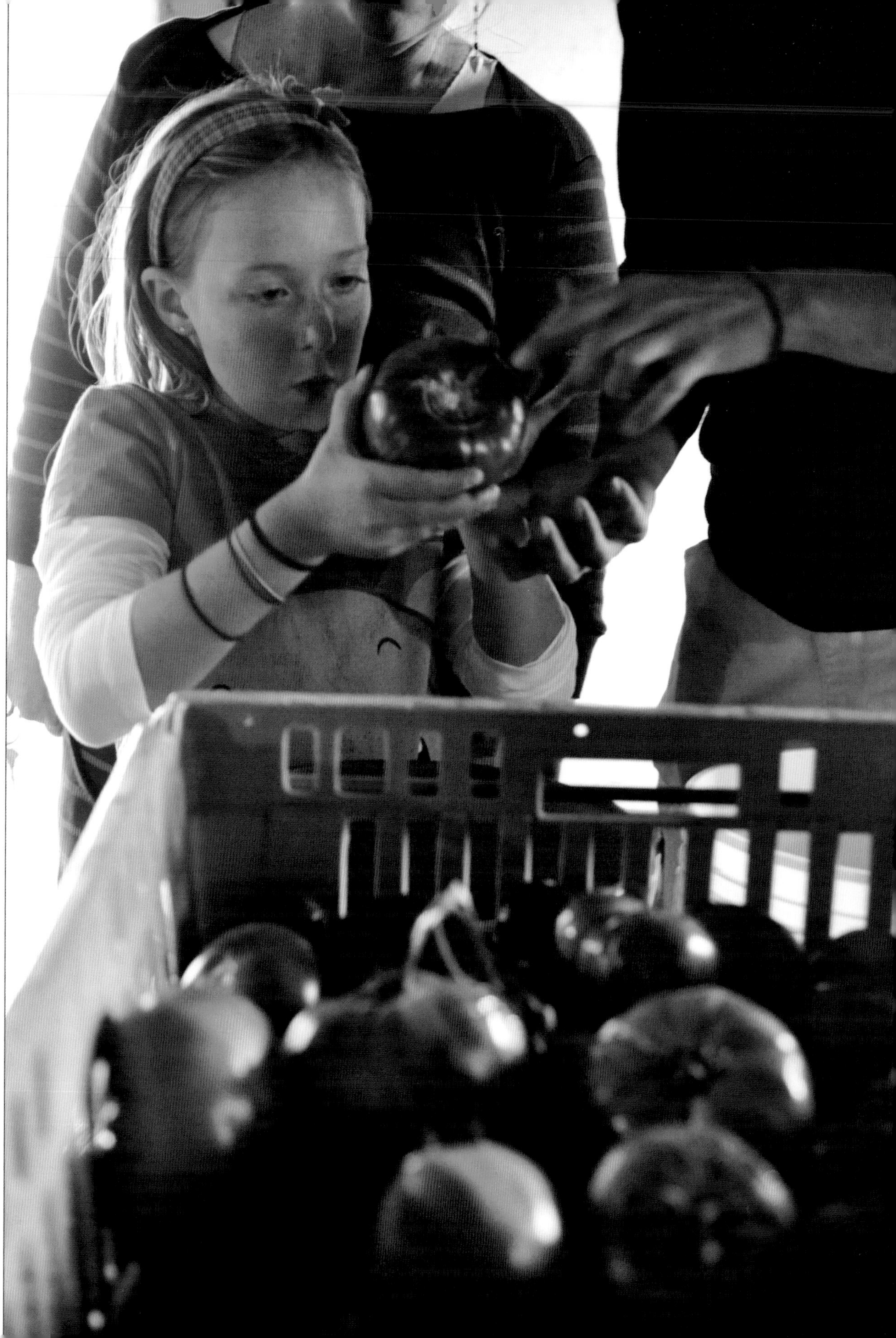

the LocalHarvest website hosts a CSA primer, "Tips for Potential CSA Members," and a database of over 2,500 CSAs, searchable by city, state, and zip code (www.localharvest.org/csa). "Community Supported Agriculture," a publication of the National Center for Appropriate Technology (online at http://attra.ncat.org/attra-pub/csa.html), discusses the history of CSAs, various CSA models and trends, and where CSA farms are located, including several specific case profiles and a survey of recent research. *Sharing the Harvest: A Citizen's Guide to Community Supported Agriculture* by Elizabeth Henderson and Robyn Van En offers a textbook approach to the subject.

Seasonal cookbooks featuring locally available produce are common in communities with CSAs. In addition, see, for example, *Local Flavors: Cooking and Eating from America's Farmers' Markets* by Deborah Madison. Those seeking to preserve their food beyond the growing season may depend on *The Big Book of Preserving the Harvest: 150 Recipes for Freezing, Canning, Drying, and Pickling Fruits and Vegetables* by Carol Costenbader; *Ball Complete Book of Home Preserving*, edited by Judi Kingry and Lauren Devine; and *Putting Food By* by Janet Greene.

See Also
Community Outreach 206

« A CSA member examines the weekly tomato selection

HOW IT WORKS

THE NEW
FACES
OF LOCAL
FOOD

STRONG COMMUNITIES PERPETUATE THEMSELVES

by instilling their values in the next generation of leaders. At a time when experts predict one-third of today's elementary school students will develop diet-related type 2 diabetes—many by the time they graduate from high school—visits to local farms and gardens may convince notoriously picky eaters to consume more fruits and vegetables. Here, after all, produce is fresh, delicious, and, best of all, dirty. And if a few of those same kids decide not just to eat vegetables, but aspire one day to grow their own, all the better.

It's good.

Mm. This one is sweet.

Green is even better.

I picked it.

He didn't pick it. He found it on the ground!

The reason why I know it's fresh is that there are raindrops on it!

At the chicken coop:

MS. KELLY: And now we're at the . . . ?

STUDENTS: Chickens!

MS. KELLY: Watch Chris's hand.

CHRIS: This is the chicken food—a lentil, a rye seed, and a bunch of other seeds and grains so they get protein. And then we have this special stuff. This is crushed oyster shell. What do you think chickens need oyster shell for?

STUDENT: When they eat it, they lay eggs!

CHRIS: It's to make the shell hard. It has a lot of calcium in it, like milk, so it makes the shell nice and hard. You guys want to see me feed the chickens?

STUDENTS: Yeah!

He's eating my food.

He pecked it off!

CHRIS: I bet he did. Look at them run!

At the henhouse:

SAARA: Do you want to see where the hens lay their eggs?

STUDENTS: Yeah!

SAARA: We're not going to go inside. We're just going to stand at the door.

STUDENTS: They're warm.

There's feathers over there!

I think they've been laying on them.

SAARA: Over there are heat lamps. They keep the chickens warm so they think it's summertime all year round. When they think it's summertime, they keep laying eggs. Otherwise they would lay eggs only one season.

STUDENTS: Can I feel the egg?

Can we hold them?

SAARA: They're very fragile.

STUDENT: Look at those boxes over there.

SAARA: That's where they sit and lay eggs. If we didn't take the eggs from the hens, they would hatch into little chicks. But we like to eat the eggs.

STUDENT: How do they get up there?

SAARA: Well, they flap. They have wings.

STUDENT: Cool!

At the carrots:

STUDENT: Look at the carrots!

CHRIS: Has everybody seen carrots before?

STUDENTS: Yeah!

CHRIS: See those tall things with the little heads on them? That's a carrot that's been in the ground for more than one year. They don't flower the first year that they're in the ground. The second year they put out the flower.

STUDENT: Look at this!

CHRIS: It's squishy.

STUDENT: Yeah!

CHRIS: Saara is loosening up the dirt around the carrots so we can get the fruit out, because the part we eat of the carrot is the fruit. And then you all are going to hold onto them, and when we get to the pigs, you can throw your greens in there.

STUDENTS: I got my first carrot.

Look at mine!

Oh my goodness! That's a great carrot!

Whoa-oh!

Look at this!

It's a witch's finger!

Look at the size of the carrot I got!

I got a real good one.

I'm going to feed this to the pig. I broke it in half. This is to the pig and this is mine.

This is mine. Look how big it is.

Can I have a bite?

CHRIS: Who had the hairy carrot? Can you hold that up? See how it's all hairy? You're not going to eat that, but roots come out of all these little starts and feed the green part. Over the winter the green part dies, but the roots stay in the ground. And next year a whole new carrot grows out.

MS. KELLY: Did anybody smell the carrots?

STUDENTS: Mm!

At the pig pen:

CHRIS: Do you guys want to feed the pigs?

STUDENTS: Yeah!

    Piggies! Piggy-wiggies! I love piggies!

        They have babies!

           I'm feeding them!

SAARA: We have one rule. What does your finger look like?

STUDENTS: A carrot.

SAARA: Yeah. So we don't want to stick our fingers near the fence, all right?

STUDENTS: Look! Feed them!

    They're big.

        They have sharp teeth!

           Last time I was here
           they were so small.

CHRIS: [Lifts slop to feed pigs] What's this gross stuff? What do you think?

STUDENT: It's slop!

CHRIS: It's slop, but it's scraps from your school lunches. We collect all the scraps from your food—stuff you don't eat and would normally just throw away—and we feed the pigs and then the pigs turn all the food you didn't eat back into food.

STUDENTS: [Mortified] Aw . . .

[Disgusted] Ew!

[Delighted] I love bacon!

SAARA: Does anybody have any questions about the pigs?

STUDENT: Do they drink their momma's milk before they eat big food?

SAARA: Yeah. They're mammals. So their mom gives them milk.

STUDENT: Look at their noses!

SAARA: Their noses are shaped like that so they can dig in the dirt.

STUDENTS: Wow!

Look at that!

Look at the mommy piggy!

How much does the big pig weigh?

CHRIS: About 550 pounds.

STUDENT: She's dusty! Why is she dusty?

CHRIS: Pigs clean themselves by taking a dirt bath. They just roll around in the dirt and it cleans them off. And Big Momma when she gets bored . . . you see that big boulder over there? Sometimes she just throws it around the pen with her nose.

STUDENT: It's really messy in there. They make it so muddy.

CHRIS: Your momma ever say your room looks like a pig sty?

STUDENTS: [Nod]

CHRIS: There you go.

STUDENTS: [Offended] Aw!

[Offended] Hey!

[Offended] Hey!

How It Works

Community Education

School gardens, farm field trips, farm and garden classes, after-school programs, and summer camps all connect young people with food and farming through direct experience in the dirt. When students learn food can come from close to home—and may even grow best with their help—their minds expand, as do their appetites for fresh fruits and vegetables.

Background

Farm and garden education programs complement traditional classroom work with a hands-on learning environment. Activities let teachers and students discover more about their food system and healthy eating habits, as well as improve their understanding of farming, gardening, and ecology.

The Garden City Harvest Community Education Program consists of three interrelated components: field trips, summer camps, and school gardens.

Field Trips

Every year, nearly 2,000 area elementary, middle, and high school students visit the PEAS Farm on one- to three-hour spring, summer, and fall field trips. Here, rain or shine, young people see the farm up close, observe growing fields of fruits and vegetables, and engage in activities and lessons that build on classroom learning.

"Using the PEAS Farm as an outdoor classroom can allow teachers and students to integrate concepts of science, math, art, history, and health in a real-life situation," says Community Education Director Jason Mandala. "Students can learn about topics firsthand, such as life cycles, farm animals, and ecology, as well as local agricultural techniques and history. These concepts are conveyed through hands-on tours and lessons such as how to make compost, the agricultural history of the Rattlesnake Valley, or discovering how large one acre is."

Joining Mandala in leading field trips are students at the University of Montana with an interest in environmental education. "I knew beforehand who my group was, what age they were, and if a teacher had requested some kind of focus, be it on insects and flowers, soil and composting, or showing them the chickens and the pigs," says former PEAS student Cori Ash. "I would pick out a couple ideas from a binder of lesson plans, ride my bike up from campus, meet with the other environmental education students, and then spend an hour and a half with the kids."

As appropriate, the young visitors help harvest vegetables, which they then sample together as a class. "You are what you eat" is a message even the most playful six-year-old takes seriously. "Seeing how food is grown firsthand gives students a direct connection between agriculture and their everyday lives," says Mandala, "and gets kids excited about healthy, nutritious food."

Summer Camps

Expanding on field trips, the PEAS Farm hosts three one-week summer day camps every June, July, and August. In each session, campers tour the farm, experience its daily rhythms and routines, help with chores, and collaborate in inquiry-based, observational, participatory games and lessons related to sustainable agriculture.

"We have a limited amount of time on the field trips, but in the summer camps, every day we do journaling, every day we do art," says Mandala. "On the last day we harvest and wash food to cook and then make a meal together. The kids set the table, we eat together, and they all wash their own dishes."

School Gardens

Garden City Harvest collaborates with the public school system, area non-profits, and trained volunteers to establish, fund, and operate a growing number of school gardens. Work in the dirt integrates curriculum inside and outside the classroom while staying on site, offering students the opportunity to learn about seasonality, ecology, life cycles, cooperative working, and the connection between the food they eat and where and how it is

A school and community garden »

Meadow Hill
Community Garden & Classroom

Est. 2003

To volunteer or for more information:
www.gardencityharvest.org
(406) 523-3663

grown. Food produced can be used in school or after-school cooking projects or as a part of special school lunch programs.

"School gardens bring to the schools the opportunity to see food grow firsthand," says Mandala. "More students can do it, and they can do it more often."

Organic Learning

Well-run farm and garden education programs take advantage of where they are, allowing ample, unstructured time to encourage exploration. "The farm is different from a normal classroom and we want them to experience the place on their own terms," says Mandala. "I don't have to be overly animated. I don't have to dress it up. Kids go crazy when they see a broccoli plant or cucumbers or celery coming out of the ground and I feed off their excitement to talk about the ecosystem and what lives and grows in the area."

Organizers lead with questions. "Lecturing doesn't work in an outdoor setting," says Mandala. "I ask questions—'What do you think is going on here? Does anyone know what this is?'—and encourage the kids to ask me questions and see if we can figure out the answers together."

Dirty hands are applauded. "Just being outside, you can see a change in kids' attitudes," says Mandala. "They're more attentive. They're more observant. Seeing and smelling and touching and tasting something new enhances their natural sense of wonder." After students see how food is grown, class, camp, and field trip leaders give them a chance to participate, planting, weeding, or harvesting—then eating. "I'm not the one pulling the carrot out of the ground and washing it and handing it to them," says Mandala. "They get their hands dirty, do it themselves, and see dirty roots transform into nice clean pieces of food."

From the fresh experience follow new eating habits. "A number of kids have been repeat visitors and they tell us that they still eat their vegetables," says Mandala.

« Q and A on a farm field trip

"We had a preschool class come up. They probably wouldn't have liked kale if their parents just gave it to them at home, but seeing the plant grow and getting to pick it themselves amazed them. Now at school they eat kale as their snack."

Reactions are immediate, but lessons learned may take years to germinate. "Working with those kids, I thought it mattered that they had pulled a carrot, for example," says Cori Ash. "At some point in their life they might reference that experience. That changed things for them. Whether every moment really made logical sense to them, the experiences themselves were broadening."

A sense of play and pleasure keeps them coming back. "We try to create an atmosphere where every activity is fun," says Mandala. "We make weeding into a game or tell stories during the harvesting." Picking peas, everyone sings and tell jokes. "It makes their experience a lot more enjoyable—and it works for adults, too," says Mandala. "Our chaperones get as excited and engaged as their kids."

Visiting the farm rain or shine »

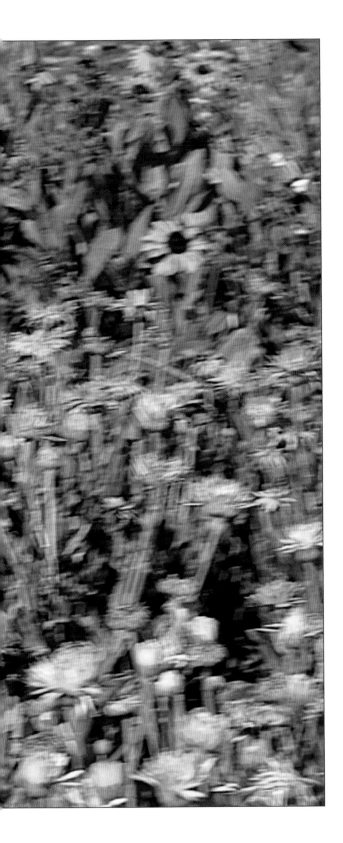

Additional Resources

The website of the Food Project (http://thefoodproject.org) shares free step-by-step farm and garden education program guides, lesson plans, and summer camp curricula, codified, illustrated, and expanded in their publication *French Fries and the Food System: A Year-Round Curriculum Connecting Youth with Farming and Food.*

The Edible Schoolyard website (www.edibleschoolyard.org), a project of the Chez Panisse Foundation, offers sample school garden guiding principles, objectives, student outcomes, and school lunch program connections, as well as recipes and lessons to use in the garden, kitchen, and classroom. Related publications include *Ten Years of Education at the Edible Schoolyard*; *Principles of an Edible Education: A Vision for School Lunch*; *Raising an Adventurous Eater: Ideas & Inspiration from the Edible Schoolyard*; and *The Garden Companion: Inside the Edible Schoolyard Classroom.*

« Taking time to smell the flowers

The National Farm to School Network supports diverse programs connecting local farmers and ranchers with school food service buyers to feed children across the country, and its website (www.farmtoschool.org) includes a discussion forum, getting-started guides, and state-by-state program profiles and statistics. Among available free publications are *Selling Strategies for Local Food Producers*; *Guide to Serving Local Food on Your Menu*;

and *Fresh from the Farm: Using Local Foods in Afterschool and Summer Nutrition Programs*.

A HEALTHY COMMUNITY IS NOT A PLACE FOR PEOPLE *without problems. Rather, it provides the right environments for those problems to heal.*

The Teenager:

Hannah Ellison

Youth Harvest Participant

"I wanted to be happy. I wanted to be healthy. I wanted to be a good person."

Every year in this country, approximately 500,000 young people enter detention centers. Not Hannah Ellison: "I was never in the court system. Because I never got caught."

I was living in Seattle with my family—we had been living there since I started fifth grade—and I became a lost, terrible person. Just drugs and running away and bad people and hurting people and ruining my whole life. And one day my dad found me, bungee-corded me, took away my shoes, chains, knives, and drugs, threw me in the back of his Subaru, and drove us all night to Roundup, Montana, where his parents were living.

I detoxed there for a week, but I don't remember being there. I had also shaved my head. So. [Laughs] If you want to know how crazy you go, you shave your head.

We were just going to pass through Missoula. My father wasn't sure what he was going to do with me. He kept threatening to put me in a foster home where they were going to put me in some other drug program. I would have just run away.

My dad went to college with Josh Slotnick and I've known their family since I was a little baby. They're good, wonderful people. Josh was like, "Geez, I hope everything turns out well, but I want you to talk to this guy, Tim Ballard." So Tim met us at the Good Food Store for lunch and my dad and I proceeded to have a screaming match in the eating area. Tim saw that we were obviously not getting anywhere because I was just *enraged*. Then we went for a walk, Tim and I, and he asked me if I wanted to be a part of Youth Harvest program, which would basically be me working up at a farm for a summer. And that's what I wanted. I was ready for my life to change.

This was spring. I started before everyone else. I was with the last group of college students before the summer program, just prepping everything, getting ready for the season, mulching, and planting early crops. That first day I remember going up there. I didn't have any clothes with me. My dad had just bought me this white dress. I still had really short hair. I had a cigarette, one of those rolled cigarettes, behind my ear, and one of the girls comes up to me: "Is that a *joint* behind your ear?" "No, it's a cigarette."

I remember walking with all those girls and talking with everybody and just having a great time. I wasn't used to being treated like a human being. I remember being really happy that first day. Really excited and hopeful. We planted onions. The first week or two, that's what we did. I planted onions for a week. I was a rock star already. Everybody was like, "Wow, you're doing great." This felt so good.

It was a couple weeks later that the Youth Harvest program started. There were four boys and me. No other girls. It was a court-ordered thing for them. We were all getting paid, but it wasn't really a choice for them to be there. It was either juvie or playing with mud. I ended up getting along really well with them, too, though. One kid got in trouble and dropped out, but they were, in general, good kids. More city kids, you know? They didn't want to get dirty.

It was a job. Tim Ballard was our boss and mentor. He was up there every day with us. We needed to be at the PEAS Farm from eight until about noon. Everybody made lunch for each other. After lunch the college students would keep working and we would go home. Pay wasn't great, but it wasn't bad either. It was more than minimum wage, which was awesome, and after a while I would get more hours and just stay up there. I worked as much as I could.

You go through life and you hope for those lucid happy moments, and I had those when I was up there. The purity of being there. Hot in the sun. Sweating my ass off, pulling weeds out of the garden. We made soil, we worked in the greenhouse, we planted seeds, we planted starts. I used the tractor. I laid out the Reemay. We prepped the vegetables. Later in the summer, we harvested the vegetables and washed them and cut them nicely and set up the table for the CSA.

There were also other parts of the program. Once a week we would get together and go for a little walk and get a treat and talk about our feelings. Normally, I would have [gives the finger] to that whole deal. But Tim Ballard was great about it. He wasn't a cheeseball. It was easy for us to talk about what we wanted for our lives.

I wanted to be happy. I wanted to be healthy. I wanted to be a good person. And I felt all that coming to me through this program. Not just because of the structure and the guidelines, but because I was so excited and because whatever I did was okay. Nobody was holding me up in the light and saying, "You must do it this way." They were like, "Well, here are your options. Take it or leave it." It made everything easy for me. I'd been ready to be an adult since I was nine years old. I wanted a lifestyle. I wanted to find out where I was going to fit. In the garden I was able to watch things grow. For me, I was able to watch my hair grow. I was able to feel a change in myself. After you've done hard drugs for a long time, time doesn't really make any sense at all. I had no idea what time was doing, but I was watching the garden and I just knew that I got up every day and I rode my bike up to the PEAS Farm and I had a good time and I hated it when the day was over.

I connected with the university students. I had a great relationship with those guys. I don't know what it was. They weren't kids, I guess. They knew their direction. They knew where they wanted to go. That's who I wanted to be around then. People who knew what they were doing. I definitely needed some guidance, I needed to be pointed in the right direction, but I wanted to walk my own path.

Everybody really liked me, and everybody was so nice. I was just so happy putting my hands in the ground, being around people who also liked putting their hands in the ground. There's something beautifully communal about it. But also fantastically original for your own personal . . . *salvation*. It's for everybody. But it's also for just you. For selfish reasons and for the greater good.

In later summer we planted all of our potatoes and they rotted. All of them. Every single one rotted in the ground. It just rained for a week after we planted them. So we all had to come up there on a day we weren't supposed to work. But we all came up. It was pouring rain. It doesn't rain like that very often, but it was just pouring, and we were trying to plant these potatoes in the mud. Generally, that'd be a pretty depressing scene. You have to redo work you've already done and it's raining and it's cold and your shoes are sticking in the mud, but we had a great time. We were throwing mudballs at each other. We were throwing rotten potatoes at each other. At the end of the day, work was done, I was covered with mud, and it was a great day. Everything rotted and it was good putting it back in the ground anyway.

Once all the hot peppers were in season, one of the Youth Harvest kids, Donny, and I, we ate a lot of hot peppers. I discovered you could actually hallucinate from eating a pepper that is too spicy. [Laughs] There are these peppers, these Bhutanese peppers, these long, reddish-orange witch's-finger-looking peppers, right? I ate the whole thing in two bites. Yellow and orange streaks started coming across my vision and I felt like—you know?—*hot*. It wasn't even spicy yet. I thought I was going to die. The next thing I remember, I'm running through the sprinklers with two cucumbers in both of my hands, just trying to douse the fires. After that I challenged everyone I saw to a hot-pepper-eating contest. "I'm just a little girl, I couldn't *possibly* eat this whole pepper, but you could do it. You're a big dude." I got to the point my tolerance was so high I was eating entire cherry bomb peppers, seeds and all, chewing them up, swallowing them. And Ari, one of Josh's friends, he ended up eating part of a pepper, and just . . . I mean, he got down on his hands and knees and we had to feed him honey and cucumber.

I had, I think, a lot of anxiety about it ending. I didn't know really what I was going to do next, and that's when I left. What happened was that the woman I was renting with, she couldn't stand living with a seventeen-year-old. I don't blame her, you know? I was so wild. So I ended up getting kicked out. I was seventeen, I was about to start school again, I was working, but no one would rent to me because I was too young. It started to get cold and I broke up with a boyfriend and I was like, "I'm trying my best and I'm still getting nothing." I just took off. I hitched a ride and went to the String Cheese Incident show outside Seattle.

For a while it felt great. There's a great romantic pull to being in that whole circle where everybody's for free love . . . and drugs . . . and wildness. It was two weeks and it started winding down and I'd been high on acid and mushrooms for a while and you come down and you're like, "Wait." You can't do it every day. You can't be high every day. You can't just party all the time. It's not always going to be summer. You realize that half these "free" hippies running around are trust kids— trustafarians is what you call them—and the other people, they go back to their jobs, they go back to their wives, you know? What was I going to do? I wanted to keep it up. I wanted to be that *Into the Wild* guy minus the dying. [Laughs] But it's just not good enough.

I thought I had burned my bridges. I don't think I told anybody before I left. I couldn't for some reason. I just left. [Shudders] I still thought the world of them. I didn't want them to think I was such a loser. I felt like such an idiot. I came down and thought, "Oh, geez, here I am burning bridges again." There's shame in it. You feel like a beaten dog. "I'm *sorry* . . . I'm *sorry*." I called my mom and said, "I think I want to go back. Could you please ask Tim if I could come back?"

So she called Tim Ballard and he, of course, said, "Yes, you can come back." So I did. I finished my summer and everybody was like, "Where the hell did you go?" And I was like [high, innocent voice], "I went to the String Cheese Incident and did lots of drugs, but I'm back now." And they were like, "Okay, let's get back to work." Nobody passed judgment.

I was glad that I went back. Summer ended and I worked to the bitter end. Until the pumpkins were out of the field and everything. In the fall I started high school. I went to Willard [Alternative High School], which is a fantastic place. For kids who cannot fit into the regular high school scene, that's the place to go. I got two years of work done in two months and graduated, and I was living in my own place by then.

I've made a lot of mistakes, but my life has been so golden since I came back to Missoula. I think there will be more good times ahead of me, but that was the golden period of my life where I found a place and I was accepted, and, beyond that, I was loved. I was so in love with everybody around me and the work I was doing. It was the best possible thing I could have been involved in. There's something to be said about home, you know? I've had lots of homes over the years, even just different houses in Missoula. I've moved probably twelve times in the past two years. But I want to stay in this town. This is where I belong. Josh Slotnick gave me a CSA share, so I go up there once a week and get my vegetables—vegetables I used to grow—and I don't know, it makes me happy. I still feel like a celebrity. I go up there and every-body's like, "Hannah!" and I'm like, "I'm here!"

Now I have that community for my baby girl, too. I'm nineteen. I was alone for the last month of my pregnancy. My fiancé was out on a fire in California. I should have gone to stay with my mom in Seattle, but I couldn't bear the thought of Maya not being born here. Someday I want to get some property out in the Bitterroot and set up my own garden and have my own business and have my babies. That's what I want for my life because of the program I was in, because of all the experience I got. That's exactly where I want my life to be—invested in all this, but my own. I'd like to grow my own food and for punishment the kids can go weed the garden. [Laughs] That sounds pretty good to me.

COMMUNITIES THRIVE WHEN EVEN THEIR YOUNGEST *and most troubled members have the opportunity to contribute their talents. First, however, those talents must be cultivated. And what better location for cultivation than a farm?*

The Counselor:

Tim Ballard

Youth Harvest Director

"I'm not looking for immediate behavioral change. . . .
What I want for them is to move into a relationship with
the farm and themselves on their own terms."

Experiential therapy often places at-risk teenagers in wilderness settings to encourage personal growth and positive relationships. Tim Ballard's bet: The same or greater change would come in the equal and opposite environment of a working farm.

After college I moved west for a summer and fell in love with the West. I stumbled into Missoula and got into the field of wilderness therapy, working with at-risk teens in experiential settings. I had just started graduate school to get my degree in counseling psychology when I ran into Josh Slotnick in the Good Food Store parking lot. I knew Josh and shared that I had an interest in doing some kind of physical outside work. He said, "Why don't you come move some pipe this summer?"

I was the farm assistant. At that point, it was just digging in the dirt, and it was only going to be a summer gig. Then, during that summer, working together, side by side, with these excited, motivated young people turning into growers, immersed in the natural world, I realized pretty quickly that I wanted to be a part of and stay a part of that experience. I was there through October, and I remember running back and forth across town between the farm and classes, showing up with dirt on my boots, smelling like I had been harvesting onions all day. I loved being in both worlds. That helped sustain me and keep my sanity in the classroom. Spring came and I signed up again. Finishing graduate school, I knew that I wanted to be a traditional therapist and do office therapy, but I also had this thought and this memory of wilderness therapy, experiential therapy, because for adolescents sitting down and talking is often not the way in. The PEAS Farm seemed like a perfect environment and container, if you will, for a transformative experience.

I started talking around town about the idea of Youth Harvest and came into contact with a woman named Ellie Greenwood, who was working with the Missoula County Youth Drug Court. Youth Drug Court is an innovative attempt at a more treatment-focused court, providing experiences that facilitate changes, not just punishment, and Ellie pulled together people from the alternative high school, the drug court, and the Human Resource Council. Everyone was in agreement that there was a unique and innovative way of reaching these kids. The alternative public high school, Willard, saw the value in providing high school credit for this experience. A forward-thinking presiding judge, John Larson, a rancher himself, got it and was willing to take risks, so Youth Drug Court provided the kids and much of the funding. And the Human Resource Council provided funding for the teen stipends, the idea being that it was going to be an employment program as well. Because the majority of the kids that came to the program were being mandated by the court, there was going to be resistance, so one way around the resistance was to pay them. The idea was to provide work experience, but also a sense of dignity.

I hire five teens each year. The majority are sixteen to seventeen years old. Four slots are reserved for kids referred by Drug Court and the other is kept for a kid who's been through challenges and would greatly benefit from this kind of experience. The idea, in part, is to have this fifth teen be a model in the mix. The other kids still struggling towards some level of change in their lives are working alongside this kid who has either been through years at a group home or years of therapy.

At the beginning and end of the season, the teens work once or twice a week after school for three hours. In the summer, they work with the PEAS program, eight to noon, Monday through Thursday. At noon the bell is rung and we sit down together to eat a meal made from freshly harvested food. Youth Harvest participants become part of this dynamic community of people only a few years older than themselves but on a very different trajectory, folks who have been successful in getting themselves into school and, for the most part, excited about what they are doing. This community provides positive informal feedback.

The teens work side by side with the students to become an integral part of the farm. They're part of something that's clearly of service to the larger community in

which they live. This helps provide them a sense of a shift in identity from one that was just troubled or in trouble or taking from society to one that is giving back. And nothing is of more tangible value than food. Everybody has to eat.

This food grows out of relationships. You show up every day and work alongside these people that you're getting to know gradually across a carrot row or spinach bed or planting onions. In this context, it's not isolating work, it's communal work. Being in it together without the pressure of a formal social situation—it's so out of context for most kids, the walls drop. There's an opening for real engagement and easier access to a sense of well-being.

In our culture, at work and recreating, there's often a disconnect from our bodies. In this work, the body is the tool and what allows for productivity. Over the course of the summer, I see confidence in the way some of these kids carry a box of produce from the wash shed to the barn or move pipe. There's an ease in the movements that wasn't there initially. To me, that translates not just to an intellectual understanding of themselves or the work, but, again, to an embodied sense or an integrative sense of what's *in* them.

I'm not looking for immediate behavioral change. I think traditionally that's what's looked for and that's just not what I'm geared for or what we're going for. There are obviously clear limits that I have to communicate, but what I want for them is to move into a relationship with the farm and themselves on their own terms. I want them to find a way to realize their strengths and capacities, and have a different relationship with their challenges and weakness, and to be more comfortable with who they are as opposed to just looking for how to please. I'm not looking for them just to become more productive members of our society.

The Youth Harvest program pushes everyone. PEAS students are curious about the teenagers. They can't just stay comfortable in their isolated college world. Many PEAS students form relationships with the kids. They find themselves in a valuable role as more mature adults and they appreciate the depth of the sometimes defiant or scattered adolescents' perspective.

TIM BALLARD

Discipline has been a real challenge and continues to be a real challenge. That's inherent in the model for us. There are varying levels of investment by the kids. Part of that is typical teenage stuff and part of it is the resistance to any mandated program. It's not a traditional job. We don't have a lot of consequences. For example, if a kid doesn't show up for a few days, I don't fire him or her; I try to understand what's going on. The court provides the strong arm. If you don't show up, then you have to do more hours at the farm or you have to do community service on top of that somewhere else. They're the bottom line, they're the law, and they make the consequences. We rely on the positive aspects of the relationship and their attachment to the farm. In this context, I'm a therapist first, and I'm very much going to err on the side of developing and preserving a relationship.

Once a week I try to meet with each kid individually and sit down. I say, "I see you're struggling. What's going on?" If someone is struggling, more focus is going to be on them than someone else that week. The issues that we work on are anywhere from the specific—timeliness,

work ethic, appropriate forms of social engagement on the farm—to struggles with parents or drug and alcohol use outside the program that affect their capacity to be on the farm. We also try to have an open-ended weekly group session where we talk about struggles outside the farm, within the farm, personal struggles, relationships, struggles that the kids might be having with some of the college students, with boredom, with weeding. [Laughs] "It's mid-July and we've been weeding for three weeks straight and it sucks!" We talk about what happens for them when they start to lose interest and motivation. In part, it's beginning to teach them how to reflect on themselves and each other in a safe context. We want to provide them with an experience that they will be able to reference later in their life as something positive.

In the last two years, an evolution of the program has been the Mobile Market delivery service for low-income seniors. It came to me that there was a disconnect for the kids between what they were doing and where the efforts of their labor would go. Even though more than half the food that we grow on the farm goes to low-income people through the food bank, there was really no interaction with the people who were receiving the food. Meanwhile, there was a real need within the senior population for fresh produce. I'd heard about a mobile grocery in inner-city Oakland. I wrote a grant to the city and got this big red van. Twice a week, the food is harvested in the morning, and, in the afternoon, a few of the kids and one staffer load up the van, and they go to two different facilities for an hour at a time, set up the table, and sell food they have grown at a subsidized rate to these low-income seniors. It's a mini farmers' market. Last year we visited two facilities. This year we've doubled it to four. Clearly, some of the benefits that have come out of it are the relationships forming across generations. [Laughs] It's never too early for the seniors to ask when the corn and the tomatoes are coming.

Successes for me are very much in the moment. A kid stopped in last week. He'd been in basic training and he came back to see his folks for a week before he was shipped off to Baghdad. He stopped out to see us at the farm and that was great. That's not necessarily the track that I would have wished for him, but he's doing well.

By coming back he said, "This was important to me." Much more common is when there is something happening at the farm, maybe a big push to harvest the winter squash, or we're planting potatoes and it's dumping rain and we're all soaking wet and it's miserable, but I look around and we're just laughing and having mud fights. Or it's overhearing a conversation. A kid has a buddy come up. I'm outside the greenhouse and he's in the greenhouse. And he's telling his friend, "Try these tomatoes, they're really good."

How It Works

Farm Work Therapy

Therapeutic, service-oriented agricultural employment immerses a diverse group of at-risk teenagers in dynamic community farms or gardens. Together each growing season, they help work the land, cultivate high-quality local organic produce, and feed those in need.

Background

Farm work therapy combines elements of work therapy, wilderness therapy, and community service. Youth participants learn responsibility and a sense of purpose, connect with the specific natural environment of a farm and with each other, and nourish fellow community members with the literal fruits and vegetables of their labors.

The Garden City Harvest Youth Harvest Program specifically targets at-risk high school students for this potentially transformative experience.

Participants

Along with an assistant, the Youth Harvest director—a professional therapist with farm work experience—employs approximately five high school students a year. Four are referred to the program by the local youth drug court. The fifth is a challenged teenager—for example, a longtime youth group home resident or therapy client— who chooses to join the program, and who organizers believe will especially benefit from a season's work on the farm.

The teenagers are paid and may receive high school class credit.

Work Therapy

Youth Harvest begins in April when participants first arrive after school at the PEAS Farm, trek across the muddy fields to the greenhouse, and begin mixing potting soil, planting seeds, and learning what it takes to be a part of a working community farm. By the time summer starts and school ends, the teens have settled into a daily rhythm with the larger adult farm community, working in the fields with university students and staff in the morning and then sharing a family-style lunch together with them around the long wooden table in the PEAS Farm barn.

As the summer progresses, the teens help weed, water, and nurture acres of plants to maturity, then harvest and deliver the abundance of vegetables to the Missoula Food Bank and organize it attractively for pickup by CSA members. Twice a week, they travel the city in a refurbished former delivery van, operating a subsidized farmers' market—called Mobile Market—for low-income, often homebound, seniors, military veterans, and the developmentally disabled.

While the corn is thinned or the squash weeded, teens and staff address daily concerns from punctuality and the understanding and development of a work ethic to the recovery from the loss of a boyfriend or the perceived insensitivity of a parent. Once a week, participants come together as a group to discuss ongoing challenges on and off the farm. The goal is to provide a safe, positive experience of problem-solving, self-reflection, and engagement with others.

A new school year begins near the height of the harvest, and the teens' service continues several days a week after classes. "The familiarity of the work and place eases them back into themselves again after a day involved in tasks that make less immediate sense," says Youth Harvest founder Tim Ballard. "We tossed pumpkins to one another across the field and gently into the back of the idle truck. We pulled armloads of onions out of the soil and hauled them into the loft of the barn, hanging them from the rafters on long lines of twine to dry for storage. We dug in search of potatoes and spaded hundreds of pounds of carrots."

The weekend before Halloween the teens set out straw bales and pile them with pumpkins. An old cider press is positioned alongside boxes of gleaned valley apples. Soon families arrive to carve pumpkins,

Gathering fresh basil for customers of the Youth Harvest Mobile Market »

press and drink cider, and warm themselves around the fire. Bare fields mean work is done for another season.

In the end, the teens walk away with "more than a wage, more than school credit," says Ballard. "What this is for each will still be growing in them long after we begin again in the spring with the next crew of young people."

Before and After

Farm work is hard, and adjudicated teenagers in particular may accept the employment only as an alternative to strictly punitive measures and traditional therapy. For these reasons, program leaders expect resistance and plan appropriate responses. Soon, however, the immediacy of a working farm's demands engages almost everyone. Working side by side with committed college students inspires the teenagers to be their best. In turn, the older—but still young—men and women invest themselves in their adolescent colleagues.

All teenagers are, in a sense, "at risk." As ever, however, the greater the risk, the greater the possibility of reward. Community outreach efforts like the Mobile Market extend new relationships and deepen teens' appreciation that they're providing a vital service to the entire city.

Healing Ties

Youth Harvest relies on the partnership of other innovative local organizations. The area youth drug court, human resource council, and alternative high school all collaborated with Garden City Harvest to create the program, and continue to help fund, operate, and otherwise support Youth Harvest, along with the City of Missoula, the University of Montana, Missoula Aging Services, the Missoula Food Bank, and generous local individuals, businesses, and private foundations.

Additional Resources

The Food Project, also mentioned in Community Education, page 136, offers a national model of engaging young people in personal and social change through sustainable agriculture, and serves as a resource center for organizations and individuals worldwide. As well as materials available through its website (http://thefoodproject.org), its publication *Growing Together: A Guide for Building Inspired, Diverse, and Productive Youth Communities* advises how to make work meaningful, how to share and uphold standards through a "straight talk" process, and offers methods of interactive teaching and learning. Included are close to 100 specific games, activities, workshops, and team-building exercises.

See Also

Student Farm   44

Community Outreach   206

SOMETIMES THE MOST VULNERABLE MEMBERS OF a community care best for one another. At a mobile farmers' market, for example, low-income senior citizens provide at-risk teenagers work experience and a sense of purpose. The teens, in turn, offer companionship, convenient affordable local food, and fresh hope for the future.

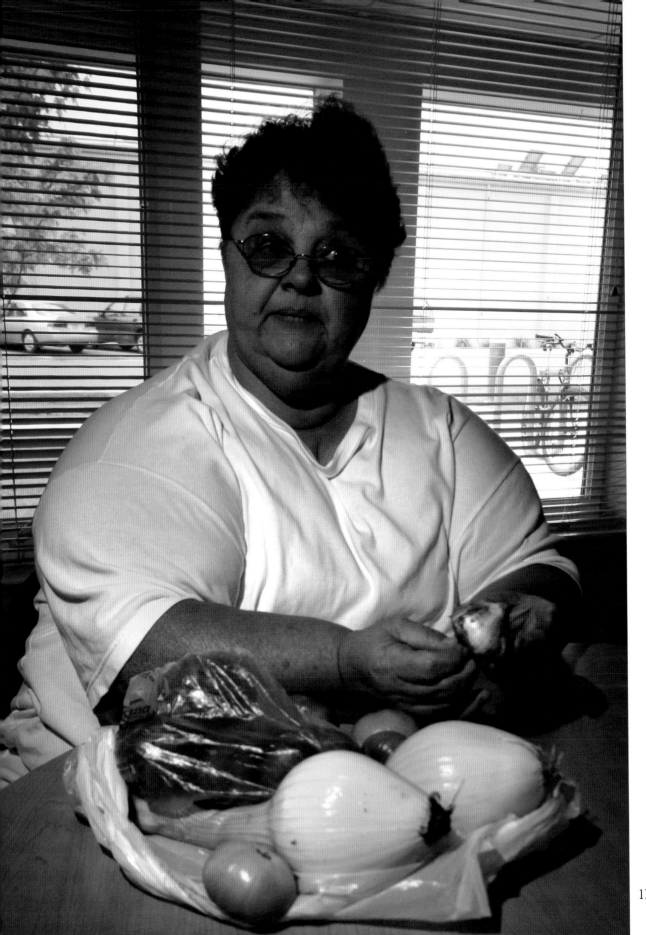

The Senior:

Vinette Rupp

Mobile Market Shopper

"I watch the season grow and fade away. They bring it right to my door."

Just before 2 PM on a sunny July Thursday, a dozen elderly men and women gather on the red-brick patio of Silvercrest Residences, a fifty-unit low-income senior citizen apartment complex built by the U.S. Department of Housing and Urban Development and managed by the Salvation Army on Missoula's near-west side. Before them a thin shamrock-patterned tablecloth weighted down with water bottles covers folding tables onto which shy, smiling teenagers in the Garden City Harvest Youth Harvest Program unload boxes of fresh local organic produce.

Basil, zucchini, lettuce, chard, cauliflower, and green beans cost a quarter. Onions, carrots, beets, and sweet peas are 50 cents. The shoppers queue, clutching canes, walkers, and empty plastic grocery bags. "There's not a cafeteria here," says Vinette Rupp. "Everybody cooks for themselves."

At sixty-two, she calls herself "the baby of the building." Her husband James, seventy, made his living as a carpenter. "When he had to retire, our income got to where it was hard to find housing we could afford," Rupp says. "We were renting a trailer in Turah, ten miles from Missoula, when Silvercrest was built, and we were the third people to rent an apartment here and the first to move in."

Last year the farmers' market started. They advertised it on the bulletin boards above our mailboxes and in the monthly calendar the office puts on our door. Music, potlucks, bingo, pinochle, a shopping outing, people coming in to take our blood pressure—anything that's going to happen during the month is on that calendar. I thought, "It's right here! I don't have to go out in the heat!"

Everybody here is on a fixed income. We're all retired. Social Security is 99 percent of our income. We get farmers' market coupons through Missoula Aging Services, but so many people don't drive and it costs $9 to take a cab from here to the farmers' markets downtown. Here they come to us and we can buy the local, the organic, the fresh, grown without chemical fertilizers and pesticides, that usually we either can't access or afford. Where else can you get a bunch of local, organic carrots for a quarter? If you go to Wal-Mart and you come here, our produce is going to beat the store's every time.

You go because you know what you're buying. You get to pick it out yourself. The kids are so polite. They don't mind you holding, touching, squeezing. When you're looking for something healthy and good for you, that's how you shop. When you go buy a tomato yourself, don't you pick it up? When you buy an herb, don't you smell it? You do if you're a cook. The potatoes and carrots and the onions these kids bring to the market don't need to be scrubbed. The Swiss chard barely needs washing. The fresh basil! Oh my, you just want to walk around and sniff it, it smells so good!

It's fun. We get to jostle with the kids and jabber with one another. I have twenty grandchildren. When these clean, wholesome, hard-working young kids come once a week, it makes an old grandma feel good. "Try the beans because they're really good," someone says. "Oh, I remember these squash from when I was a little kid," says someone else. Talking, we exchange recipes. Until I told them, people didn't know that you could stew zucchini. Beets are one of my favorite vegetables, but I didn't think you could have them raw and that they'd be good or even edible. Someone chopped them into sticks small enough to eat and they were awesome.

It means the world to me that it comes from Missoula. I'm one of seven siblings and we grew up right here in this neighborhood. I remember when my grandmother came to live with us and Daddy made $1.50 an hour. Back then, gardening was a way of life. That's how everyone but rich people fed their families. Thirteen dollars a day raised seven children and supported ten people because we had corn, pumpkins, pole beans, peas, carrots, cucumbers, tomatoes, raspberries, and strawberries, and everything went into canning jars.

Now my husband and I will get in the car after dinner and just drive around town to see the gardens growing. At first look I thought, "Oh my, they must have a huge family!" I came closer and saw the sign: "Garden City Harvest." We take our friends from the apartments with us and say, "See, this is where it comes from." You go out into the Rattlesnake or Orchard Homes area or the North Side and see these huge gardens growing everything under the sun,

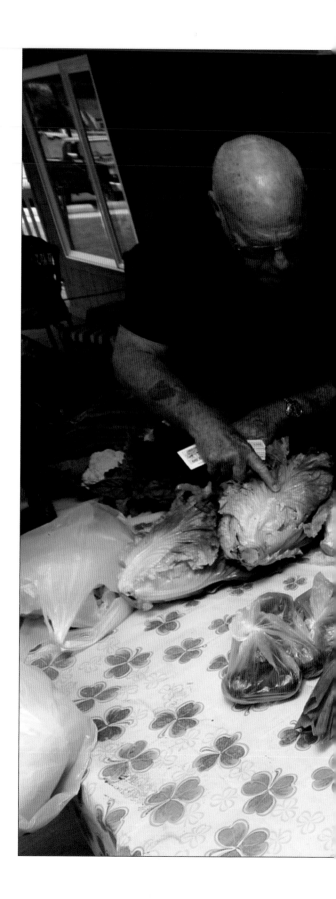

and you wonder who does this? Then you watch and see the whole neighborhood show up and work.

We're proud to be able to have these people come to us. They're here every Thursday afternoon for a good hour. At least fifteen to twenty of us show up every week. Some come early, others straggle in, and it's easy in, easy out for everybody. Over a summer at the market, we recognize the kids and they recognize us, too. They say, "Hey, how you feeling?" A lot of us don't get to see our grandchildren as often as we'd like. To see these happy young people involved in their community and proud that they can deliver food to us gets our old hearts cooking. We started monthly themed potlucks. For example, August is Fair Days because that's when we have the Missoula County Fair, and we'll have soups, sandwiches, and salads using produce from the market. The women are all good cooks and some of the bachelors would give their teeth for a home-cooked dinner. My sisters and I learned to cook watching Momma. She made baked beans with bacon, homemade white bread, and fried chicken with potatoes. On your birthday, everybody was at the door to sing to you and at dinner that night there was always a cake.

The farmers' market keeps me happy. As soon as it starts, I get a sense of the seasons: first lettuces and the carrots, then basil and other fresh herbs, then the tomatoes come in, and as the summer grows we have fresh peas and beans. In the fall, they bring apples and pumpkins. Because a lot of the ladies like to decorate, after the harvest is done they even bring the stalks. I watch the season grow and fade away. They bring it right to my door. Come fall, I've got my pumpkin and my squash, which gets me through Thanksgiving dinner. Come Christmastime, though, I'm fixing meals, thinking, "Man, wouldn't it be great to have a plate full of fresh tomatoes?" Spring comes and I watch the calendar and the bulletin board.

Just the other day we had a potluck and ice cream social. One of my friends made a phenomenal quiche using Swiss chard, zucchini, and onions from the market. Teddy, the service coordinator, made a salad with market lettuce, beets, cucumbers, onions, carrots, and green and red peppers. It was just astounding how good it was. Everything was crisp that was supposed to be crisp. The green peppers shined. She had little julienned pieces of beet, so you had the beautiful pink and purple colors in there with the green. Such good food brought back the home cooking that I had as a child. It brought back the potlucks that we used to have at church. It was just awesome. [Laughs] You should have been there.

USUALLY THE WORDS "ORCHARD" OR "GARDEN" *in a real estate development refer to the past rather than the future. But center a new neighborhood around local agriculture and residents rediscover our society's roots.*

The Single Mother:

Kim Markuson

Orchard Gardens Resident

"Things really picked up. People started to go out there. They got into it. Neighbors would start talking about vegetables: 'It's good,' 'It's so yummy,' 'It's crunchy,' 'It's fresh,' 'I love it.' That's not a conversation I normally would have had."

Her mother died when she was twelve and her eldest brother when she was sixteen, but Kim Markuson graduated salutatorian of her high school class. "I got good college scholarships," she says, "I was going to go on and do great things."

Then freshman year, first semester, her father died, too. "I was like, 'Forget life.' School was overwhelming. I quit for six years. Now I'm trying to get back on track."

She is thirty years old. Her daughter Laney is four. Last summer her best friend became homeless, so she adopted the woman's seventeen-year-old son.

Home is the thirty-five-unit Orchard Gardens development, built by a local nonprofit, homeWORD, committed to providing "safe, healthy affordable housing using sustainable methods and promoting strong communities." All residents earn no more than 50 percent of the area median income. Two acres of the nearly five-acre site are community gardens facilitated by Garden City Harvest.

When I first moved here I wasn't too involved with the garden. To be honest, I thought, "Oh that's cool, but I'm not big on organic food. I really don't care." [Laughs] I'm Salish. I grew up in St. Ignatius, Montana, where my tribe is from. It's a small town—1,000 people, if that—and people are really into sports like the basketball team. People aren't into organic. In Missoula everybody was like, "You're so lucky—you've got that garden!" I was like, "Oh yeah. The garden thing. I don't even use it."

What happened was that the kids started going out to the garden. There are four of us single moms right along this row. We all moved here at different times, but living alone is sometimes scary and we watch out for each other's kids. All of our daughters are four or five years old. All of them just loved to go out in the garden with [Orchard Gardens Community Gardens and Neighborhood Farm Manager] Sarah [Bortis]. They would do that all summer long. I started talking to Sarah because Laney would go play. I would see her out and I would go out, too, and say, "Is this okay?"

As I got to know her, Sarah would tell me what she was doing. She put fliers on my door to say, "We're getting ready to have our community garden plots. If you're interested, call me." She had informational meetings. She offered us the "volunteer for veggies" deal where you volunteer a certain amount of time for a certain amount of pounds of vegetables. I always meant to do that—I always had the best of intentions—but I'm in school, I'm raising kids, and I'm just tired at night. I didn't want to go garden. It would probably have been good for me, but I just didn't have the time. The whole summer went and I never volunteered.

Then the next spring and the summer, Sarah planted more and more. On Thursday nights she set up a little farm stand in front of the community barn. At first not many people went. Orchard Gardens residents are pretty open-minded, but we were all just learning what she does and getting comfortable with her and with each other. There are single people and elderly people. There are students. There are traditional, two-parent families and single moms like me. You might have seen someone every day and not known them or even said hi.

As more time went on, though, things really picked up. People started to go out there. They got into it. At that little stand neighbors would start talking about vegetables: "It's good," "It's so yummy," "It's crunchy," "It's fresh," "I love it." That's not a conversation I normally would have had. [Laughs] I didn't normally talk to people about vegetables. But in the summer, there were always people out at the farm stand or working on their plots. Kids played everywhere. You met people.

It appealed to me because where I'm from you talked to everybody no matter what. Families had close ties. When my mom and brother passed away, I grew up with the kids of my foster mother and her sisters. All of my aunts raised us together. Like home, this is semi-rural. It's quiet. There are a lot of low-income people, but the kids can play safely. When I got vegetables, I would share with my neighbors. One time I had to leave on a trip, so I gave away three bags of vegetables. My neighbors were so happy getting good food right out of the ground. Once you're drenched in it, you realize food tastes so much better when it's in season.

Last summer Sarah started doing food shares. She explained to me that if I paid $200, I'd get a certain amount of seasonal groceries each week from the garden. I just had to go pick them up and I didn't have to do any of the gardening. The best part was you could use your food stamp card. Every week I could afford to buy fresh organic vegetables and salads to feed my family. I thought, "This will be perfect."

Every Monday, Sarah set up a little shop in the back of the community barn. At first she gave us one or two bags of lettuce, so I would cut up all these different varieties of lettuce and mix them together. I made a big salad and put it in Ziploc bags and it would keep fresh all week. Then at the peak of the season in August you got three or four bags packed with fresh veggies. You took as much as you needed. You could feed a family of four for a week.

Because I got a lot of cabbage, I made a lot of coleslaw. I would grab cilantro, garlic, onions, and different kinds of tomatoes—orange ones, yellow ones, red ones—and make fresh salsa and tomato sauce. I mixed it up and tried a million varieties of hot peppers. I tried leeks. We had blue potatoes! I had never had a blue potato. [Laughs] I was like, "Oh, crazy. Oh my gosh. These are just beautiful."

It was so cool learning how to cook with all those different foods. Everything Sarah grew I would try in recipes. I had never cooked with bok choy, but I made big stir-fries because stir-fries are easy. I made roasted root vegetables. Sarah would tell me how to cook stuff I wasn't used to eating. She would get specific, saying, "Oh you can do this with fresh herbs, that with potatoes." I made pesto and I'd never made pesto before. I'd never had gnocchi before and we made it from scratch.

My daughter loved it. Fresh vegetables and salads became her favorite snacks. Laney became a tomato freak. She would always ask for fresh tomatoes. If they were bigger tomatoes, she would ask me to cut them up for her. If they were cherry tomatoes, she would go help herself. It was to the point where she couldn't come in the garden anymore! [Laughs] It was too hard for her not to pick vegetables when she was sitting out there. It was like putting a kid in the candy store and saying, "Don't touch that candy. Don't look at it."

How would I describe my life right now? Okay. This is important. Right after he moved in with me, my foster son totaled my car. It wasn't his fault—it was a complete accident—but my insurance didn't cover the car and we've had a hard time since, recovering financially. That almost made me go over the edge. You wouldn't believe how your life falls apart when you don't have transportation. I'm going to school, trying to make sure the kids get to school, trying to take care of the finances, and trying to graduate. I'm reading my syllabi, figuring out how to do my homework, and getting the car thing figured out. It's manageable, but it's winter and I don't have any fresh vegetables and that's stressing me out. I'm serious. [Laughs] I really miss those fresh veggies. Pre-packaged bags of lettuce mix suck.

Spring will come. The kids will finish school and I'll graduate. I'm majoring in communication studies and I want to go to law school. Now I take it for granted, but the garden changed me. I think of how to be more healthy. I appreciate the taste of fresh food. Living here, my body got used to eating fresh vegetables. All summer long I could go into my fridge any time and make a salad. Now it's winter, but I'm already looking forward to the sugar snap peas. Sarah can grow a mean tomato. I can still taste those vegetables now.

**MORE THAN 36
MILLION AMERICANS,
INCLUDING**
*over 12 million children,
are "food-insecure." For
the hungry, the gift of
local food provides not
only a needed meal,
but also something rarer
and as valuable: a sense
of ownership in their
community.*

The Homeless Shelter Chef:

Jesse Schraufnagel

Poverello Center Food Insecurity Programs Director

"There's a presence in the community of all these little gardens. People see them and know them. It was rewarding for them to know that maybe they helped grow something, which in turn came back here, which in turn they were eating."

"Meals Served: 4:30 AM to 7:30 AM, 11:30 AM to 2:00 PM, 5:30 PM to 6:30 PM."

Each year Garden City Harvest donates more than 7,000 pounds of produce to western Montana's largest homeless shelter and soup kitchen, the Poverello Center. Here, in a former three-story family residence in downtown Missoula, a kitchen, dining room, and food pantry share space with bathrooms and showers, a medical clinic and clothing room, laundry and mail facilities, staff offices, and sleeping quarters for seventy. "Sixty percent of the people coming in and eating meals here actually have an apartment or motel room or house," says Jesse Schraufnagel. "They're not homeless. They use this resource just to help them get by."

There are no requirements to eat here. All we ask of folks is that they come in sober. In 2007, I served 102,000 meals. In 2008, that number jumped to 117,000. That was an all-time record. Now we consistently see above 10,000 each month. People have problems with housing. They worry about whether to pay for gas or meds or food. Funds start to run out towards the end of the week and the end of the month. If a Friday falls on the twenty-ninth or thirtieth or thirty-first, I'm not surprised to serve 200 people for lunch and 150 for dinner. We do three meals a day and we have one range with two ovens in it and one warmer.

How I started is I saw an ad in the paper looking for a person to work nights. I did that for two years, and in that time I saw three separate kitchen managers come and go. In college I majored in archaeology, which is a far cry from cooking in a soup kitchen, but I thought: "I can do that." Working the night shift, 7 PM to 7 AM, was wearing on me. Although I had never had any training in cooking or even worked a job doing that, I was pretty confident that I could handle it. All I can tell you is that for the first three months everybody helped me immensely. People would come in and say, "Can we have meatloaf?" I would say, "You get in here and you show me how to make it!"

Garden City Harvest is a perfect example. I started in the kitchen in September 2006, toward the tail end of the growing season. I was scrambling around, trying to figure out how to cook for 350 people, and we started getting inundated with squash from River Road Garden. Maybe "inundated" is a bad word, but we got 600 pounds of squash. [Laughs] I didn't know what to do. I honestly didn't have any idea how to cook it. We set it all on the dining room tables. [Laughs] We used it as decoration.

Greg Price came in. He was a chef at one point. He takes a lot of pride in his produce and he wants to see it used in the best way possible. He saw squash sitting on every table and said, "You should bake that squash. You shouldn't use it as decoration. Here, I'll tell you how to cook it."

He did and I was amazed. We just chopped and prepped and baked the squash with butter and a sprinkling of pepper and garlic powder. Everybody loved it. I couldn't cook it fast enough. It was just flying out of the pan. Folks told me, "That squash tastes just like my mom used to make it. Where did this come from?"

When I told them it came from Garden City Harvest, they took ownership. Maybe our clients don't have cooking facilities at their small apartment or motel room, or they're homeless, but there's a presence in the community of all these little gardens. People see them and know them. They really appreciate being able to have high-quality, local, organic produce. People came up to me and said, "Did this come from the PEAS Farm? Did this come from River Road Garden?" They'd tell me little stories about how they'd stopped by and chatted with someone there once, or volunteered some time and helped out. It was rewarding for them to know that maybe they helped grow something, which in turn came back here, which in turn they were eating. That opened my eyes.

Since then, every spring I look forward to seeing Greg come through the door. I'm usually scrambling around in the kitchen, elbow deep in a casserole or fixing soup or something, and I see the back door open and Greg standing there with a big box of

produce. First thing in the spring, he brings us early spinach and lettuce for salads. As the season goes on, we get broccoli and cauliflower; we get corn, beans, peppers, and peas; we get collard greens, kale, and chard; we get 500, 600, 700 pounds of potatoes and onions from the River Road Garden and the PEAS Farm. Those are staples for us. Every day we make twenty gallons of soup. We cook vegetables in almost anything you can imagine. Today, for example, I had planned to make beef vegetable soup, so yesterday volunteers chopped up peppers, carrots, celery, cauliflower, broccoli, mushrooms, and onions, and we started a stockpot with beef. I got here at six in the morning and I dealt with my stockpot, straining out all the stock and reserving the meat on the side, getting the stock boiling again, and adding my vegetables. That's part of lunch and dinner for 250 people.

The Poverello Center is thirty-five years old, but we live day to day. Where food is coming from means a lot. We get ground beef, frozen chickens, pastas, beans, and canned vegetables through the state and the federal government, but everything else comes in as a donation. One day we could get fifty cases of milk; for the next three weeks we may get nothing. Even getting things from grocery stores around town is a food rescue program: We're rescuing things from going to the landfill. Apples and peppers have spots on them, or they're slightly damaged, or they're not at the peak of their freshness.

Everything we get from Garden City Harvest is fresh. They picked it that morning and drove it right here. Folks who come here generally have health problems. A lot don't have the opportunity to cook a vegetable or prepare a square meal. A lot eat only one meal a day. They'll come in for lunch and then they'll move on. It's important to me to pack as much as I can into each serving. I'm not going to force anybody to eat anything, but if I put out a pan with canned green beans next to a pan with fresh green beans, 99 percent of the people take the fresh green beans. I won't even cook the peapods that Greg brings us. I just put them out raw for people to eat and enjoy. Even in entrees and soups, fresh food adds so much more flavor and so many more vitamins, minerals, and nutrients.

Our clients can tell. They don't say it out loud, but I know because when Greg drops off produce, I hear them say, "Wow, look at that ultra-green broccoli!" "This squash is beautiful and it doesn't have a spot on it!" One day we got a huge box of collard greens from Garden City Harvest and a guy from the South, I think he was from Tennessee, he came in and said, "I'm going to show you how to cook the best collard greens ever." We chopped them all up and everybody loved them. Like the squash, it went faster than I could even cook it! It really surprised me. The folks that came and ate that day recognized how fresh it was. Word spread very rapidly. Everybody else jumped in line and had to have some.

Garden City Harvest and the Poverello Center have developed a partnership. I enjoy the relationship. I know we take pride in cooking and feeding people and they do, too, in providing fresh food. Every summer Greg brings in something new. Once he brought in a different variety of sweet peppers that he was trying out and they looked like they would be blisteringly hot, but they were the sweetest peppers that I've tasted in my life. I just ate one raw and it was the most delicious pepper that I had ever eaten. That's special to me. That feels good: People giving me so much that I want to give something back.

I rely on Garden City Harvest. With them I know that I will consistently have delicious fresh produce. I can't be certain of some of these other means of getting food. Towards the end of last winter we had a cold snap when it was twenty below. We had 102 people for a week. When all the beds filled up, we pulled out mats and moved the tables out of the dining room and we slept people on the floor. We weren't getting any fresh produce through our commodities program or from the grocery stores. We came to a point where we were almost even out of canned vegetables. It was right about that time, the springtime, when Greg showed up with his first batch of produce. It saved me. I knew that I could count on being able to feed people for the rest of the summer.

We really do care here. Taking care of each other embraces our sense of community. Last summer we served our two millionth meal. We had a guy here traveling to

Seattle from Florida. Someone there had told him, "When you go through Missoula you have to stop at the Poverello Center because the food is unbelievable. When you get there, ask for Jesse. He will take care of you."

I'm still more than willing to learn. Because I'm not a chef by trade, if I get a request and it's something that I don't know how to cook, I'll step aside and say, "Why don't you come on over here and show me?" I get satisfaction from someone telling me, "Thank you. Thank you for the meal." They don't even have to tell me it was good. That's fine. [Laughs] But I enjoy being able to take everything that comes in the door and utilize it in a way that people appreciate. At least five times a day I hear someone walk by the food line when I'm in the kitchen and say, "Jesse, that was awesome. Thank you."

CORN FLAKES, TUNA FISH, PEANUT BUTTER, *and frozen pizza: leftover, damaged, and donated food items—most of them highly processed—have stocked food bank shelves for decades. Yet if eating fresh fruits and vegetables is best for health and well-being, shouldn't community farms serve those who need their produce most?*

The Food Bank Officer:

Aaron Brock

Former Missoula Food Bank Development Director

"For any food bank, the foremost objective is to provide food to folks who are hungry. We can modify that objective by saying, not just food, but really high-quality, fresh local organic food, grown with our clients in mind by people we know."

Without restrictions, anyone may visit the brightly painted downtown store and warehouse of the Missoula Food Bank as often as once a month for a three-day supply of emergency food assistance. Supplementing non-perishable staples and food items donated by area supermarkets, restaurants, and residents are 20,000 to 25,000 pounds of fresh, organic fruits and vegetables grown expressly for the food bank each year by Garden City Harvest. Every ounce matters: In hard times, the food bank serves as many as 130 families a day.

"Missoula County has roughly 100,000 residents and we average over 12,000 unduplicated clients each year," says Aaron Brock. "That means, walking downtown, one in every eight people you see is coming through our doors."

When I joined the staff at the food bank in 2003, I started with every misconception. You see folks in Missoula hanging out under the bridge or as you pull off I-90. They're holding the cardboard sign that says, "Have a buck?" I had that in my head. I remember looking at the numbers: "*12,000 separate individuals coming through the door each year? Come on! There's not 12,000 panhandlers in Missoula!*" I didn't realize people coming to the food bank look exactly like you and me.

There are so many people living and making it month to month, but the budget is tight. You may be a single person who has a full-time job and the car broke down. You're making $8 an hour, and you need your car to keep your job, so you put $120 into repairs and that's your grocery money. You may be someone facing a medical crisis. Hard-working parents come in and they both have jobs, but they don't have health insurance, and their kid broke his leg. That's not something you can just roll with. You've got to seek medical care, but your tight budget breaks. Folks pull up in their cars. Guys come in wearing a tie from a job interview. With outreach programs, we serve more and more of our elderly, and I can't believe some of their living situations. There was a widow of ten years whose income was her husband's Social Security: $670 a month. There's a poverty line and then there is way down where this person has just been surviving. Every year, 40 to 45 percent of the clientele that we serve are under eighteen years old.

The mission of the food bank is not just to give away food to people in need, but to provide the highest quality of food possible. Someone who is facing hunger, they're not hungry because they're hungry, they're hungry because they're in poverty, because they don't have health care, because they're sick, because they're out of work, because they don't have transportation, because they don't know how to grow their own food. With the food bank, we're not solving problems other than your immediate problem of not having food to feed your kids. Until you feed your kids, though, it's really difficult to move on with other pieces of your life. When we can

AARON BROCK

partner with Garden City Harvest, providing local food that's grown for us, fresh from the farm, in a sustainable way, that's never been touched with pesticides, there's no question that that's the best way to serve you.

Garden City Harvest makes it easy. Typically every day during the growing season, they show up in their red truck. There might be four or five or six kids in there along with a staff person. They pile out, grab boxes of produce harvested that morning, weigh the boxes for record-keeping, then help put the food right out on our shelves, so people who need it can take it. During the growing season, our produce cooler looks every bit as abundant and inviting as that at any local grocery store. We've got two big levels on it, twelve to fourteen feet long, and right away you see fresh heads of lettuce and cabbage recently sprayed down with beads of water on them. The kale and chard are vibrant and the carrots and cucumbers are crisp. We have beautiful corn, tomatoes, peppers, and basil; onions and potatoes; and green and yellow squash.

Things that are easy and recognizable fly off the shelf. Lettuce is unintimi-dating. Tomatoes, carrots, potatoes, and onions go fast. When it's something like green peppers that people have grown up eating and they see it here, and they see it's beautiful, they're excited. A lot of our clientele aren't otherwise exposed to local produce as part of their everyday diets and we've got volunteers who hang out by the cooler saying, "This scary-looking thing is kohlrabi and here's what you do with it. It's easy to cook, you'll feel good after eating it, and your kids will even like it. Just try it." At the front, you'll be met by volunteers to help you box up your groceries. Often they say, "I don't see any produce in here. Did you miss it? Do you want it?"

Someone on a tight budget, when they're going to the grocery store, they're not in experiment mode. They're thinking, "How do I squeeze the most I can out of my last twenty dollars?" Because a squash is intimidating-looking, someone in that position is not going to buy one at a grocery store. Here, people pick them up and say, "Is this just for decoration?" "No," we say. "Here's how you cook it. It's easy."

Whether those folks come back or not, they know how to use it for the rest of their lives. I remember one person who came and grudgingly accepted bok choy because a volunteer by the produce cooler talked it up, then they came back the next time and said, "Wow, that was so good in my stir-fry. Do you have that again?"

The food bank and the Garden City Harvest have been working hand in hand for twelve years. The relationship is symbiotic. Garden City Harvest can focus on farming because we have the volunteer staff to rotate the produce, to keep it looking good, and to advocate for people to take it if they don't know what it is. Whether it's college kids, staff, or participants in the Youth Harvest program, when they come to the food bank and load food and stand next to the folks in true need who are taking it home and are grateful for it, they see how the fruits of their labors make the community better. There's something profound about discovering having something to give, however modest it is, and when you're involved in every step from the time the seeds are planted to the time the food leaves the food bank in the hands of a hungry family, it brings it full circle.

It's special that Garden City Harvest grows high-quality food specifically to feed hungry people. Those who walk through the doors at the food bank are not an afterthought. It's grown for them, and I think that's unique. Certainly it plays a big role in how we see ourselves in the community and how we feed people. The food bank can't go and pay market price to put organic peppers on the shelves, but we know that Garden City Harvest consistently provides between 20,000 and 25,000 pounds of produce every summer. That's predictable. That's important. For any food bank, the foremost objective is to provide food to the hungry. We can modify that objective by saying, not just food, but really high-quality, fresh local organic food, grown with our clients in mind by people we know—by friends and neighbors.

In some ways, although the food bank's work is joyous work and it's a vibrant place to be, there's something inherently sad about any food bank. You're seeing folks who are absolutely in need and who have had to overcome all kinds of barriers of pride to reach out their hands for something as basic as sustenance. Long before the first food banks started in the 1960s, people relied on their neighbors for help in hard times. What happens with Garden City Harvest and the food bank is neighbors feed neighbors again. It's addressing our needs directly and trying to do so in the highest possible way. I recently left the food bank to join the Missoula YMCA as its development director, but I still volunteer here and with Garden City Harvest. A person can walk into the food bank without food and leave twenty minutes later with groceries, including food grown within the community. Just to have groceries you have a little more self-esteem. And, hopefully, you've also felt tangible human kindness.

How It Works

Community Outreach

When community farms and gardens draw the participation of teenagers, seniors, military veterans, the developmentally disabled, the homeless, the hungry, and low-income individuals and families, they demonstrate that local organic food may be anything but elitist. Far more vital, they foster the sense of connection necessary to improve the conditions of contemporary life for all.

Background

D iverse outreach efforts bring the benefits of community farms and gardens to an entire city. In reaching out, community members fulfill their own and others' basic needs for sustenance, companionship, and a positive purpose and sense of self.

Garden City Harvest community outreach programs engage and serve teenagers, seniors, military veterans, and the developmentally disabled; the homeless and the hungry; and low-income individuals and families.

Serving Teenagers, Seniors, Military Veterans, and the Developmentally Disabled

Using fresh Garden City Harvest farm produce and a refurbished delivery van, teenage participants in the Youth Harvest Program operate a traveling subsidized farmers' market—Mobile Market—at housing complexes for low-income seniors, military veterans, and the developmentally disabled.

Former Youth Harvest participants frequently serve as neighborhood farm or community garden assistants in subsequent growing seasons. As well, food grown at the River Road Neighborhood Farm helps supply local youth homes, many of whose residents in turn volunteer their labor at group work projects.

Serving the Hungry and the Homeless

Garden City Harvest farm sites grow tens of thousands of pounds of food a year to feed clients of the Missoula Food Bank and Poverello Center homeless shelter and soup kitchen. The local organic vegetables are picked fresh and often delivered daily. Over 40 percent of those served by the Missoula Food Bank are under eighteen years old. As many as half of Poverello Center clients are military veterans.

Serving Low-Income Individuals and Families

Garden City Harvest locates all community gardens in low- or mixed-income neighborhoods, the better to serve residents without money to buy their own fresh local organic food or land on which to grow it. At one of the organization's newest gardens, for example, plots serve the neighborhood, the local Catholic parish that donated the land, and homeless families living in adjacent transitional housing.

More comprehensive yet is Orchard Gardens, an innovative low-income housing development built around a straw-bale barn and new neighborhood farm and community gardens. Here, in addition to enjoying a weekly subsidized farm stand, locals can "volunteer for veggies," trading labor for fresh vegetables, or sign up for reduced-price community garden plots or CSA shares. The barn has entertained "Real Meals" cooking classes combining inexpensive local food with communal meal preparation, and the site and others in the Garden City Harvest network host weekly after-school children's activities centered around local food and farming.

Growing Community

From farms and gardens grows food, and from food grow relationships. Site visitors and volunteers range from kindergartners to seniors, adjudicated teens to tenured college professors, and families and young professionals to youth home and homeless shelter residents. A sense of welcome lets individuals help themselves, and, for recipients of the produce, its local origins are a source of pride.

Unloading fresh farm produce for the Youth Harvest Mobile Market »

Additional Resources

The Community Food Security Coalition (CFSC) combines training, networking, and advocacy to build strong, sustainable, local and regional food systems that ensure access to affordable, nutritious, and culturally appropriate food to all people at all times. Presentations, handouts, guidebooks, and reports, many available free of charge through the CFSC website (www.foodsecurity.org), include *Whole Measures for Community Food Systems: Values-Based Planning and Evaluation*; *Sowing Opportunity, Harvesting Change: Community Food Projects in Action*; and *What's Cooking in Your Food System?: A Guide to Community Food Assessment*.

Civic Agriculture: Reconnecting Farm, Food, and Community by Thomas A. Lyson and *Growing Home: The Guide to Reconnecting Agriculture, Food, and Communities* by Joanna Green and Duncan Hilchey further explore opportunities for inclusive sustainable community development through local agriculture.

Garden City Harvest
Missoula Montana
523-FOOD (3663)
"Putting the gardens back into the Garden City"

Afterword

How Garden City Harvest Works

Garden City Harvest's Mission Statement:
1. Grow and distribute healthy food to low-income people.
2. Offer education and training in ecologically conscious food production.
3. Use our sites for the personal restoration of troubled youth and adults.

Background

Over 90 percent of the produce eaten in Montana is shipped in from out of state. Yet a century ago Missoula earned the title "The Garden City" by producing fruits and vegetables for much of the surrounding region. Garden City Harvest was founded in 1996 to revive the tradition of producing local food for one's community, especially the 20 percent of Missoulians who live in poverty.

"Food security, as we decided, meant two things," says Garden City Harvest co-founder Josh Slotnick. "One, people would have access to food. They would know they could eat tomorrow and the next day and the next. Two, the production of food would be similarly available. The way we produced food now would also enable us to produce food in the future."

With temporary land from the University of Montana, a USDA Community Food Project grant, and strong support from a diverse group of committed individuals, businesses, fellow nonprofit organizations, and local government entities, work in the dirt began. In its first season, Garden City Harvest produced more than 57,000 pounds of fresh vegetables, most distributed through local emergency food agencies. In its second and third season, the organization grew and gleaned more than 60,000 and 74,000 pounds of food, respectively. Today, food grown averages upwards of 100,000 pounds a year.

Each season, Garden City Harvest has increased the number and scope of farm and garden programs as well as individuals and groups served in its community.

Programs

Garden City Harvest meets its mission statement with four programs:

- PEAS Farm, a 9.75-acre student farm run in partnership with the University of Montana Environmental Studies Program, whose produce supplies the Missoula Food Bank, Youth Harvest Mobile Market, and a CSA.
- Community Gardens and Neighborhood Farms, where local residents can rent a plot and grow their own vegetables; "volunteer for veggies," trading labor for fresh produce; join a CSA; and help grow food to feed Mobile Market shoppers, area youth home residents, and homeless shelter, soup kitchen, and food bank clients, among others in need.

- Youth Harvest, a work therapy program run in conjunction with the local youth drug court, human resource council, and alternative high school to provide a nurturing environment, employment, and therapy for troubled youth.
- Community Education, whose school gardens, farm field trips, summer camps, farm and garden classes, after-school programs, and other activities educate area youth and adults about their food system, social and ecological community, gardening and farming, and healthy eating habits.

Power from the People

Garden City Harvest staff includes an executive director, PEAS Farm director and facilities manager, Youth Harvest director and assistant, community education

« **"Wintergreens" winter community gathering and fundraiser dinner for Garden City Harvest** ⅀

director, community outreach director, neighborhood farm managers, community garden organizers, garden assistants, and a financial and office manager. They are overseen and supported by a twelve-member board of directors, with further funding from and partnerships with local businesses, nonprofits, charitable foundations, government offices, the public school system, and the University of Montana.

Most of all, however, the organization relies on thousands of individual participants—farmers and first graders, counselors and troubled teens, foodies, seniors, single mothers, and more—to cultivate a modern Garden City.

"Our edible open spaces are safe and near people, where they can grow their own food, where they can teach their children about where food comes from, where they can touch the soil," says Community Gardens Director Tim Hall. "It's the fullest sense of community and . . . whether individuals or organizations volunteer to grow the food or to take the food, they're helping us support our mission."

A sense of ownership starts with engagement, and Garden City Harvest invites every resident to gather, celebrate, work, and learn on the land. Public events include concerts, classes, lectures, readings, and city-wide celebrations.

At local food- and farming-themed fund-raisers, the community gives back: $35 pays for the summer rent of a garden plot; $100 buys fuel each month for the tractor at the PEAS Farm; $150 funds electricity to run the irrigation pump; and $250 purchases eighteen weeks of vegetables for a low-income family. Each farm and garden welcomes volunteers and hosts work parties either to build or maintain infrastructure or to accomplish major group tasks such as planting, weeding, harvesting, and food storage. End-of-year potlucks of local food dishes celebrate the successful harvest, and similar spring events usher in a new growing season.

Call it agriculture-supported community. "People drive by, they walk by, they come here, and they congregate," says Josh Slotnick. "It's part of the public sphere and the public dialogue and culture." Whether there to work, play, pick up food, or enjoy the view, visitors appreciate that their local farms and gardens can lead the nation. "They don't say, 'Oh, that could happen in California, it could never happen

Preparing stuffed squash blossoms at Garden City Harvest's summer "Field to Plate" community dinner and fund-raiser »

Garden City Harvest co-founder Josh Slotnick offers salad to guests at the "Wintergreens" dinner »

« Making
contact on the
farm playground

here,'" says Slotnick. "They read about [local food] and they're like, 'Oh, yeah, we've got that, too.'"

To join them, find or found your own local farm or garden. As River Road Neighborhood Farm and Community Garden Manager Greg Price says, "To fully get what community means . . . get out and participate."

Additional Resources

For more information about Garden City Harvest and its programs and their participants, or to make a tax-deductible contribution, visit its website (http://gardencityharvest.org) or contact its offices at:

Garden City Harvest
103 Hickory Street
P.O. Box 205
Missoula, MT 59806
(406) 523-FOOD (3663)
gardencityharvest@gmail.com

« Final visit for the season

Acknowledgments

It took a community to write this book.

Susan O'Connor first proposed the idea of a book about Garden City Harvest, then championed our efforts through more than a year of development.

The staff at Garden City Harvest gave us complete freedom to observe and record their hard work. In particular, Josh Slotnick and Joellen Shannon signed on from the very beginning and encouraged others to do the same.

From day one, Chad Harder was more than a lead photographer—he was a full partner in this project, and his instincts, intellect, and attitude never failed to improve my own. In the final stretch, Sepp Jannotta stepped forward to deliver great shots on a tight deadline. Kashia Yurek transcribed a dozen interviews, Karen Slobod provided invaluable initial layout and design expertise, and Zander Ault helped me visualize our Garden City. Bill McKibben's foreword is the best opening to a book about food and community an author could imagine.

Two books directly inspired this one: *On Good Land: The Autobiography of an Urban Farm* by Michael Ableman and *Harvard Works Because We Do* by Greg Halpern. Both authors guided and encouraged me through the early stages of *Growing a Garden City*, as did Carl Smith, Jane Smith, Linda Matthews, Arnie Kotler, Kermit Hummel, Jim Mairs, Joni Praded, Rob McQuilkin, Seth Fishman, Emily Takoudes, Kisha Schlegel, Anna Lappé, and Annick Smith. It was through Annick that I met my editor Lilly Golden and the talented team at Skyhorse Publishing.

Publication of this book was made possible in large part by generous grants from the Prop Foundation of Missoula, Montana.

My greatest debt is to my interviewees, who shared their personal stories of transformation, and to Crissie McMullan, my wife and partner, who encouraged me every day to share the concept and principles of a Garden City with the world.